Dublin
1847

CITY OF THE ORDNANCE SURVEY

Frank Cullen

Dublin City
Baile Átha Cliath

Acadamh Ríoga na hÉireann
Royal Irish Academy

First published in 2015 by the Royal Irish Academy (www.ria.ie), Irish Historic Towns Atlas, 19 Dawson Street, Dublin 2, in association with Dublin City Council (www.dublincity.ie), Wood Quay, Dublin 8.

This edition printed 2019

ISBN 978-1-908996-35-0

Irish Historic Towns Atlas series editors: Anngret Simms, H.B. Clarke, Raymond Gillespie, Jacinta Prunty; consultant editor: J.H. Andrews; cartographic editor: Sarah Gearty; editorial assistants: Angela Murphy, Jennifer Moore, Frank Cullen.

British Library Cataloguing-in-Publication Data. A catalogue record is available from the British Library.

Printed in Poland by BZGraf S.A.

5 4 3 2

In memory of Paula

my wife, best friend and mother of our beautiful son, Daniel

CONTENTS

CONTENTS *continued*

This book is one of a number of ancillary publications to the Irish Historic Towns Atlas. These are intended to make available material relevant to published atlas fascicles. This volume accompanies Irish Historic Towns Atlas, no. 26, *Dublin, part III, 1756 to 1847* (2014) by Rob Goodbody. It presents and examines extracts from the large-scale Ordnance Survey town plan for Dublin city (1847), which was a crucial cartographic resource in the fascicle.

Dublin 1847: city of the Ordnance Survey is a joint publication between the Royal Irish Academy and Dublin City Council. The author and editors are grateful to Frances McGee, Hazel Menton, Honora Faul and Paul Ferguson for advice with regard to the large-scale town plan and to Andrew Bonar Law for his generosity with regard to illustrations.

Anngret Simms, H.B. Clarke, Raymond Gillespie, Jacinta Prunty
Editors, Irish Historic Towns Atlas, Royal Irish Academy

PREFACE

In any major European cartographic operation two contrary pressures can generally be identified: economy keeps regional maps small; topography makes urban maps large; the obvious result is for towns to be mapped at a larger scale than the surrounding rural areas. It was not therefore unexpected when the Ordnance Survey was preparing for its Irish commitment in 1824 that the director, Thomas Colby, should suggest mapping towns at double the six-inch or 1:10,560 scale recommended for the country as a whole. Once the new survey had begun there was further discussion about what urban scale would suit the government's official valuators for whom all the Survey's non- military Irish maps were primarily intended. The chief valuator, Richard Griffith, wanted four feet to a mile, and it was Colby who suggested increasing this to five feet, which at exactly ten times larger than the six-inch would make it easier to use the Ordnance Survey's plotting instruments. In due course Colby's view prevailed. Plans of this unwieldy size were of little interest to the ordnance establishment, and they seldom figure in departmental correspondence. Archivally speaking, urban mapping remained a second-class citizen in the government's cartographic community for some time to come, and Dr Frank Cullen must be congratulated on unearthing a number of new facts about the coverage of Dublin in this series.

The publishing of these and other Irish Ordnance Survey maps in the 1830s and early 1840s was a responsibility not of the Board of Ordnance in London but of the lord lieutenant and his government in Dublin. Their belief, judging by the course of events, was that the nation's capital city deserved its own all-purpose large-scale map, whatever might happen in other towns. Clearly such a map should be made generally available, although the Survey took care to test public opinion by first publishing just one of its thirty-three constituent sheets as an experiment. Binding this sheet in the same volume as the six-inch survey of County Dublin (1844) was a magnified equivalent of the marginal inset town plans familiar in early private provincial and county maps.

To what extent and by what means Colby's officers adapted their survey methods to this demanding new framework is hard to say. For instance, how much precise observation was devoted to the plausible-looking lawns, flower-beds and garden paths of the Dublin plan? Here is a difficulty familiar to historical map-users: how to distinguish rep-

resentational verisimilitude from conventional symbolism. For the most part the Dublin map manages to avoid this problem, accommodating with apparent accuracy information that previous cartographers would not have tried to squeeze into a traditional urban format. Examples were the exact shapes of individual buildings, the divisions between adjacent houses, and the precise widths of streets. These improvements opened up their own possibilities. Expanded street widths made possible the inclusion of drains, sewers and water mains, as well as the numbering of houses. Less generalised outlines allowed the depiction of interior lay-outs in buildings of public importance, a spectacle that was to dominate the finished map. Elsewhere minor names and other verbal identifications — pump, weigh house, crane, ball court etc. — could be multiplied apparently without limit.

All these issues emerge from the introduction to Dr Cullen's book and from its numerous illustrations. His main text makes several further contributions. One, inspired by recent progress in Irish architectural studies, is to add a verbal component of walls, pillars, gateways and upper storeys to the Ordnance Survey's ground plans of public buildings. In the resulting three-dimensional word-picture, refreshingly, a value-judgement can sometimes be allowed its place. At the Richmond Female Penitentiary, for example, 'The massive seventeen-bay, three-storey, unrelenting facade advancing right to the edge of the street was designed with one effect in mind: to intimidate. No gravel walkways or shrubbery greet the incoming prisoner, just cold grey calp'.

The author's widest appeal, however, will probably be in his analysis of the real-life uses to which the city's urban furniture was put. He is particularly informative on hospitals, prisons, orphanages and other institutions, but in the end we are given a balanced view of an increasingly public-spirited city still exhibiting well-marked regional contrasts of poverty and wealth. At the same time Dr Cullen's interpretation of the phrase 'in 1847' is unpedantically liberal. His temporal dimension appears in frequent reminders of the Victorian city's antecedents and their socio-economic effects — the Wide Streets Commission, the Act of Union, the Napoleonic wars, Catholic emancipation, the coming of the railways, and finally the famine and its associated population movements. Nor does the narrative stop pre-

FOREWORD

cipitously at any particular year. Where a historical process continues after the 1840s — as with the development of port installations to the east of the city — we can follow its course at least as far as the next appropriate natural break.

One way to form an overall impression of this book is by reference to the twenty-two thematic headings in the 'topographical information' section of the Royal Irish Academy's *Irish Historic Towns Atlas*. How many of these categories can be applied to the 1847 map and to Dr Cullen's commentary? The answer is most of them. Altogether he provides a well-balanced history of early nineteenth-century Dublin, grounded in topographical facts without being slavishly dependent on them, and written with sensitivity and enthusiasm. It is a pleasure to introduce his work.

J.H. ANDREWS
Consultant editor, Irish Historic Towns Atlas

FOREWORD

The Ordnance Survey town plan for Dublin comprises 33 separate sheets each 920 x 610 mm in size. The maps were produced at a scale of five foot to one mile (1:1056) and were published in 1847. The map extracts included in this book have been taken from a set of sheets in the National Library of Ireland, prints and drawings department and they are reproduced courtesy of the National Library of Ireland. This set of maps has been scanned, joined and cropped to provide the extracts. Each detail has been sized according to the area under discussion and the scale of enlargement or reduction for each is not given.

The map extracts are numbered 1 to 45. Numbers in bold in the text provide a cross-reference to a relevant extract. The commentaries loosely follow a clockwise direction from the Royal Barracks in the north-west to Kilmainham Gaol and Court House in the south-west and this can be followed on the index map inside the front cover.

In the introductory essay (part I), building and street names are standardised to those used in Irish Historic Towns Atlas, no. 26, *Dublin, part III, 1756 to 1847* by Rob Goodbody. In the text that accompanies the map extracts (part II), the forms of name as given on the 1847 town plan is used.

ABBREVIATIONS
OS   Ordnance Survey
NAI   National Archives of Ireland
NGI   National Gallery of Ireland
NLI   National Library of Ireland
NUI   National University of Ireland
TCD   Trinity College Dublin

EDITORIAL NOTE AND ABBREVIATIONS

LIST OF ILLUSTRATIONS

PART I: Introduction

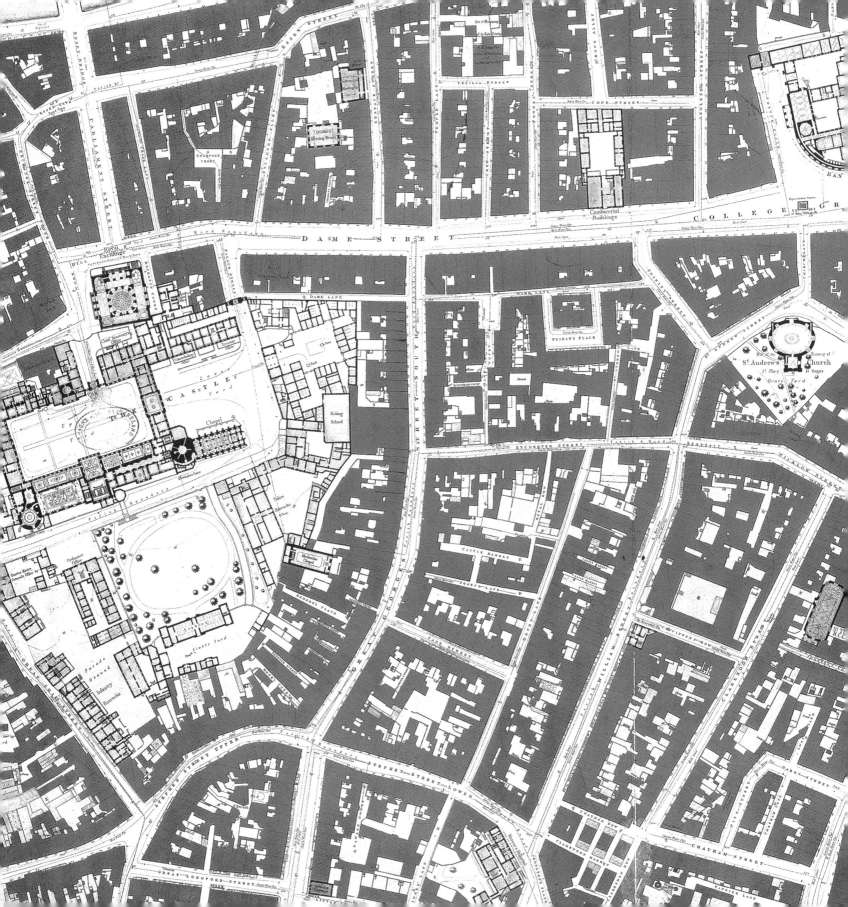

THE ORDNANCE SURVEY
AND THE DUBLIN TOWN PLAN OF 1847

When famine struck Ireland in 1845–7, Dublin — 'placed in the bosom of one of the loveliest bays in the world' — was ranked among the finest cities in the British Empire.[1] On leaving the bay to enter the city, visitors could not help but be impressed by the River Liffey, spanned by eight elegant bridges and lined on either side with three miles of busy spacious quays.[2] From Carlisle Bridge (O'Connell Bridge, see **29**) — the centre point of the mid-nineteenth-century city — the vista opened out in all four directions taking in Sackville Street (O'Connell Street, see **13**) to the north, Westmoreland Street, D'Olier Street and College Green (see **30**) to the south, while to the east the view was dominated by James Gandon's Custom House (see **16**), and westward, beyond the Metal Bridge, could be seen the dome of the Four Courts (see **9**), with the Phoenix Park receding in the distance. Owing to the work of private developers such as the Gardiners and the Fitzwilliams, the city that was surveyed by the cartographer John Rocque in 1756 had by 1850 become a modern metropolis with railed garden squares and stylish buildings lining its many new, wide and airy streets. This was the Dublin surveyed and mapped in immense detail by the Ordnance Survey, a result of which was the publication in 1847 of the five-foot to one mile maps of the city, the primary source for the present book. The plan, comprising thirty-three separate sheets, lays out the city for all to see and represents an extraordinarily detailed depiction of the topographical landscape in 1847, with comprehensive coverage of urban themes including streets, religion, defence, administration, primary production, manufacturing, trades and services, transport, utilities, health, education and entertainment.

SURVEYING THE CITY AND PRODUCING THE MAP

The Ordnance Survey was established in Ireland in 1824, on the recommendations of a select committee chaired by Thomas Spring Rice, to report on the best means of providing a general survey and valuation of Ireland. For decades Ireland had laboured under an archaic system of local taxation whereby occupants of rateable properties paid a local tax based upon the value of their property. As no map of the country at a standard scale existed, inconsistency could often arise in the valuation of properties since units of measurement varied from place to place.[3] Having conducted its investigations for a period of three months, the Spring Rice Committee reported on 21 June 1824 with the recommendation that Colonel Thomas Frederick Colby, director of the Ordnance Survey in Britain, should take the necessary steps to ensure that a survey of Ireland at a scale of six inches to one mile should proceed without delay.[4] Mountjoy House in the Phoenix Park, Dublin, was chosen as the headquarters of the Irish survey and Colby appointed Major William Reid as his deputy in Dublin. In 1828 Reid was succeeded by Lieutenant Thomas Larcom[5] who remained as Colby's deputy in Dublin until 1846. Under Larcom's direction and inspired by his energy, Mountjoy House became a hive of activity in the 1830s and 1840s and so strong was Larcom's influence that the six-inch maps became known colloquially as 'Larcom's maps'.[6]

Fig. 1, opposite: OS, printed town plan, Dublin city, sheet 21, 'Castle Sheet', 1847 (NLI).

INTRODUCTION

The all-Ireland survey, carried out between 1829 and 1846, was a highly co-ordinated endeavour, conducted according to the principles of what Colby referred to as his 'system'.[7] Colby's system was based upon division of labour. The surveyor who carried out the chain measurements was entrusted with surveying and measuring only, and did not plot his own work. That task was given over to the plotters who were subdivided into groups, some with responsibility for plotting the main lines of the survey and others responsible for plotting the detail. Similarly, the drawing and tracing were also given to those specialising in this field. Through this system each man became an expert in his own particular task and worked independently of his colleagues, thus ensuring less margin for error.[8]

By 1837 almost half of the country, including Dublin city, had been surveyed.[9] The survey of the city commenced on 15 May 1836 and was conducted by the Ordnance Survey's E Division, which was divided into five separate districts, each under the control of a commissioned officer of the Royal Engineers. Lieutenant G.F.W. Bordes was given responsibility for overseeing the city survey while Lieutenant Henry Tucker[10] was put in charge of the county of Dublin. The remaining three officers took charge of parts of the surrounding counties including Meath, Kildare and Wicklow.[11] At least twenty surveyors comprising an evenly-balanced mixture of non-commissioned officers of the Royal Sappers and Miners, and civilian surveyors, known as 'Civil Assistants', were involved in the initial fieldwork that took the men into the wealthiest and poorest parts of the city. From the elegant town houses on Merrion Square to the tenement slums of St Michan's and St Catherine's (see **24**, **39**), gardens, yards and perimeter walls were measured in detail. Venturing into such unhealthy parts of the city was a risk that came with the job. In December 1836 Corporal William Tozer was struck down with a sudden attack of fever while involved in the survey of St Catherine's parish. He died in August 1838 quite possibly as a result of this attack.[12] Although empowered with special authority to enter private property, disputes and misunderstandings between the Ordnance men and members of the public were anticipated on account of the minute nature of such a large-scale survey. In a letter written one week before work was due to begin, Bordes requested to know how he might act in cases where persons refused to admit his surveyors into their back yards.[13] Unfortunately the result of Bordes' request

must remain unknown since the original correspondence does not survive. Nevertheless, by April 1837 most of the streets and buildings in the city had been measured in detail as the surveyors worked their way methodically from parish to parish.

During the winter of 1836 two three-man teams were actively involved in surveying the Merrion Square district of the city. Privates George Brook and William Baker of the Royal Sappers and Miners headed each team and their respective schedules, judging from the evidence presented in the field books, appear to have been quite hectic with both teams working through the weekends. On Saturday 27 November Brook, along with civil assistants William McEniney and M. Smith, were busy surveying Merrion Square North, Denzille Street and Holles Street, while on the following Sunday they had moved onto the south side of the square. The other team headed by Baker was taking measurements in the tenements at Verschoyle Place just off Lower Mount Street on 21 December, and even on Christmas Eve they were working on the east side of Merrion Square.[14] Similar teams operated throughout the city in 1836 and 1837, and their work, recorded and plotted at a scale of five feet to one mile, provided the basis for the published six-inch and five-foot maps of 1843 and 1847 respectively.

As each district in the city was surveyed work quickly commenced on the plotting of that particular area on a five-foot scale. By October 1836 the parishes of St Michael's, St John's, St Werburgh's, St Andrew's, St Audoen's, St Nicholas Within, St Bridget's and the liberty of St Patrick's had all been fully surveyed and plotted, with the remaining twelve parishes at various stages of completion, the exception being St Luke's which had yet to be commenced.[15] As each five-foot plot was completed it was followed by preparation work on the manuscript plans for that particular area at both the six-inch and five-foot scale. The six-inch manuscript plans (often referred to as the 'fair plans'), and the five-foot manuscript town plans were completed in 1839 and 1838 respectively. Throughout the various stages of preparation the examination department played a crucial role in checking each plot and draft for omissions, errors and accuracy, thus ensuring the integrity of the overall process.[16] Owing to motives of professional pride the first of the Dublin sheets was engraved and published in 1840. Sheet 21, known as the 'Castle Sheet', received such a positive response from all quarters that it not only encouraged the publication of the remaining

INTRODUCTION

Dublin sheets, but of other towns also (Fig. 1, p. 2).[17] By 1843 the manuscript sheets, originally completed in 1838, had been revised to record any new changes in the landscape and the process of preparing for publication the 1847 town plan of Dublin city was well under way.

The five-foot to one mile map of Dublin city published in thirty-three separate sheets in 1847–8 was over twelve years in the making. During this lengthy process scores of individuals played their part in its production. From the surveying and plotting of the streets and buildings, to the pen work, colour, ornamentation and writing of the maps, each team was responsible for its own specific task, yet in some cases individuals moved from section to section as they gained in experience. This is apparent in the original records where names involved with the initial six-inch survey reappear on the manuscript town plans drawn up in 1838 and revised in 1843. Civil Assistants Matthew Clinton and A. McLachlan, for example, whose names were both connected with the survey of St Thomas's, St Werburgh's and St Andrew's parishes, also contributed to the colour and ornamentation[18] of some of the large-scale manuscript sheets of 1843.[19] Purvis, McKeown and Dickson, all civil assistants and all responsible for the plotting and penning of the fair plans in 1837, also worked at all stages on the preparation of the 1838 manuscript sheets. McKeown, for example, who carried out the ornamentation work on the Merrion Square sheet, was given responsibility for the penning, colour, ornamentation and writing of sheet 9 which included the Richmond Female Penitentiary (see **24, 4**).[20] This overlap between personnel does not of course apply to the published 1847 map as the Survey's engravers never worked at any other task.[21] All of this points towards an impressively co-ordinated venture with teams of variously skilled individuals working to a precise plan. Even accepting the senior role played by both Colby and Larcom, and to a lesser extent Captain John Cameron who succeeded Larcom in 1846, it would be misleading to apportion credit to any one individual for the publication of the 1847 map of Dublin city.

The 1847 map covers the part of the city inside the two canals in addition to the eastern port area north and south of the Liffey. The detail is exquisite with all aspects of the built environment depicted, from rivers, canals, docks and city basins, to streets, squares, parks and orchards. Public buildings such as barracks, prisons, workhouses and asylums stand out owing to their style, scale and location in what were previously undeveloped suburbs. Also highly visible are the many churches and chapels in the mid-nineteenth-century city, in addition to the major public buildings such as the Custom House, Dublin Castle, Royal Exchange, Four Courts, General Post Office and Trinity College (see **16, 31, 9, 13, 28**). A striking feature of the map is the level of detail captured in the overall plan. Pumps, water mains, sewers, toll gates, trees, shrubberies, house numbers and even flower beds in individual gardens are recorded meticulously. It would be astounding to think that surveyors went so far as to copy such minute detail from every garden plot in the city. However, this was not the case. Private Brook's field book for Merrion Square, for example, contains pages of highly technical chain measurements and calculations, which to the untrained eye bear no resemblance to the finished map.[22] Even the actual square itself appears as a complicated mass of chain measurements within a large rectangle, nothing like the neat landscaped depiction on the 1843 and 1847 manuscript and printed maps, which both show two gates on Merrion Square East as opposed to the three gates shown in the corresponding field book.[23] On Merrion Square South the houses, though loosely drawn, are faithful to the proportions of the building with precise measurements noted along the perimeter walls. No garden shrubberies are depicted in these field drawings, just the word 'garden' written in each specific garden plot. While the maps do exhibit some degree of creativity in this respect, particularly in the Phibsborough district (see **5**) with its numerous neatly-decorated garden plots displaying a wide variety of symmetrical motifs, such creativity did not go unchecked since all completed drafts were taken out into the field for examination by the aptly-named 'field examiner', whose job was to ensure that each draft represented as accurate a depiction of the area as was possible.

Some features of topographical interest, though recorded in the surveyor's field book, remain unnamed on the printed map. In the rear garden of 20 Lower Mount Street, for example, the field book shows an outbuilding identified by the word 'hothouse'. Although the same hothouse is depicted on the manuscript and printed maps for this particular address, it is not named and subsequently unidentifiable. It might therefore be presumed that similar structures were commonplace in the more affluent neighbourhoods, though not necessarily identified on the finished map.[24] One of the more remarkable features of detail on the map is the depiction of ceiling work in the city's high-

INTRODUCTION

profile public buildings. In extract **14**, the Music Hall located on Abbey Street Lower serves as a useful example in this respect. The contemporary illustration of the building's interior included in this extract shows four large skylights in the ceiling, which correspond nicely with the depiction of the same building on the map.[25]

From the beginning of the Irish operation Colby had been adamant that the Survey take no responsibility for identifying property boundaries on the ground, content to leave this task to the boundary surveyors working in advance of the Ordnance men.[26] Within the uniform topography of a city with its streets of terraced housing and walled gardens, the Ordnance men were less dependent on the boundary surveyors for identification of individual properties, yet they still took great care to insert division lines in building blocks and to number each and every house. One of the final features to be added to the map was contour lines. The process of contouring, advocated by Larcom in 1839–40, had already been in use by military topographers on the Continent. While earlier maps of Dublin such as Rocque's *Exact survey* of 1756 and Thomas Campbell's *City of Dublin* of 1811 use hachured lines to depict the uneven surface of the land, the Ordnance Survey's more scientific use of spot heights and contour lines was especially innovative and expanded the utility of the published map (see **24**).

For those working in the Phoenix Park's Mountjoy House, 1846 was a frantic year. After a bitter dispute between Colby and Larcom, the latter was dismissed from the Ordnance Survey.[27] The shock waves were felt far and wide and Captain John Cameron was brought in to succeed Larcom.[28] With the impending publication of the five-foot map of Dublin, the timing was poor, but there would never be a good time to replace a character of Larcom's stature. At this late stage the task of representing sewers, water mains and contour lines on the map had yet to be completed. In February 1847 Cameron requested that the Commissioners of Paving make available to the Ordnance Survey a map depicting all the sewers known to them in the city. Although the commissioners obliged, the map was on too small a scale, thus leaving them with no alternative but to send a man out with the Ordnance officer to point out the location of sewers around the city.[29] By May Cameron was forwarding sample copies to Lieutenant Colonel Lewis Hall, Colby's successor,[30] for inspection and approval, and proposing that fireplugs, turncocks and gratings also be engraved.

Hall, anxious to make a personal contribution, returned the maps with his instructions.[31]

Although the five-foot printed map of Dublin is a representation of the city in 1847, the engraving of the water mains and sewers on the sheets continued into the following year with demand for the prized maps increasing from all quarters. In February 1848 the town clerk, on requesting for the corporation a copy of the map on which the sewers and water pipes had been laid down to assist in a local enquiry, was informed that only fifteen of the thirty-three sheets were completely engraved and that the remaining eighteen would take two weeks to complete.[32] In June Captain Yolland, deputy director of the Survey in Britain, requested copies of all the five-foot sheets completed, as did the public health officers assigned to the various parishes of Dublin.[33] Perhaps the most telling factor in the popularity of the Dublin map can be seen in the directive sent out from Mountjoy House in December 1853 by Colonel Henry Tucker (formerly of E Division) banning the making of tracings from the maps presented to the library of the King's Inns.[34]

DUBLIN ON THE TOWN PLAN OF 1847

Dublin as depicted on the Ordnance Survey map of 1847 was a complex urban site. In the wake of the great city-wide survey of 1836–7 the population of the capital stood at 232,726, a considerable increase from the figure of 150,000 when John Rocque mapped the city in 1756.[35] Population growth led to physical expansion, the extent of which by 1847 was clearly visible in the diminishing rural spaces remaining within the Royal and Grand Canal boundaries enclosing the municipal district. On the 1847 map the topographical landscape was that of a modern affluent capital city with wide and spacious thoroughfares linking elegant squares and gardens. Adorning the streets were impressive neo-classical public buildings designed by eminent architects such as Edward Lovett-Pearse, Thomas Burgh, Thomas Cooley, James Gandon and Francis Johnston. New canals and docks show the extent of infrastructural improvement with the Liffey walled in on both sides from the North Wall to the King's Bridge (Seán Heuston Bridge). Notwithstanding its commercial prosperity, dramatic demographic growth in the first half of the nineteenth century exacerbated an existing problem for the government and municipal authorities, as poverty, disease and crime became

INTRODUCTION

pressing issues that required attention. The impressive detail of the 1847 town plan depicts well the proliferation of medical, penal and charitable institutions addressing these problems in the post-1800 city (see **3**, **34**, **38**, **40**, **42**). Security was also a primary concern both leading up to and following the union of 1801, the growth and extension of new and existing gaols and barracks reflecting this anxiety (see **1**, **4**, **8**, **44**). In many ways mid-nineteenth-century Dublin's topography was a product of the Act of Union, the most graphic topographical expression of which was the sale of the parliament house in 1802 to the Bank of Ireland (see **30**).

(Grattan Bridge), increased traffic within the municipal district demanded further improvements to the street plan. The first scheme initiated by the commissioners was the laying out of Parliament Street in 1757 to open up access from Dublin Castle northwards towards Capel Street and, via Great Britain Street (Parnell Street), to Rutland Square (Parnell Square) and Sackville Street Upper (O'Connell Street Upper) (see **11**, **13**). This was followed with the widening of Dame Street and College Green and the southward extension of Sackville Street in the 1770s and 1780s. With the construction of Carlisle Bridge in the 1790s the only requirement was a thoroughfare linking the south city to the newly-built bridge. Rather than building one street the commissioners built two. Westmoreland Street was laid out in 1799 to complete the circuit from the south-west to the city's grandest and widest thoroughfare, while D'Olier Street — laid out in the same decade — provided the link eastwards via Great Brunswick Street (Pearse Street) after 1812 (see **29**, **31**).[36]

Fig. 2: Carlisle Bridge and Westmoreland Street, *c.* 1850 (private collection).

Commercial prosperity is reflected well on the map, particularly in the growth of the port. The development of the Custom House complex on the North Wall quay in the 1820s with its new docks and warehouses, along with the new Grand Canal docks on the south side of the river, attest to a growing economy in the years following the Napoleonic Wars (see **17**). Under the watchful eye of the engineer John Rennie, the lands adjacent to the Custom House were transformed to enhance the trade of the port. Two new docks, George's Dock and the Inner Dock (the former named in honour of King George IV's visit in 1821) provided new berthing facilities in line with the growing demand for quay space. Great bonded warehouses were also constructed adjacent to the docks, giving shape to the early nineteenth-century port.[37] At the eastern extremity two patent slips located at East Wall (see **22**) demonstrate a small ship-

The legacy of the Wide Streets Commissioners established in 1757 is captured for the first time in the comprehensive street plan, with new streets and bridges opening up circulation within and around the old city core and shifting the emphasis eastwards (Fig. 2, above; Fig. 3, p. 8). Mobility in the city had been a problem for the authorities dating back to the early eighteenth century. Although this problem had been addressed in 1753 with the erection of the new Essex Bridge

INTRODUCTION

building industry. More emphasis, however, was put on ship repairing rather than building as the century progressed. Indeed this was the main purpose of the new graving dock designed by port engineer George Halpin senior in 1859. Also under Halpin's supervision, as the name would suggest, a deep-water hole known as Halpin's Pond was dredged on this site directly south of the patent slip depicted on the map.[38] Its purpose was to give shelter to vessels awaiting quay space farther upriver. With the arrival of the young Bindon Blood Stoney as assistant engineer in 1856 this primitive initiative would develop during the final decades of the nineteenth century into one of the most technically advanced deep-water basins in the world.[39] As the port expanded, the vacant North Lotts area east of the Royal Canal, conspicuous in their appearance as newly-reclaimed enclosures, very quickly industrialised after this period. The 1847 town plan therefore captures the industrial port of the nineteenth century on the verge of a great period of major infrastructural transformation that would continue into the next century.

The growth in trade obviously had a knock-on effect for the financial and economic well-being of the city. This is noticeable in the mid-nineteenth-century topography, with numerous new public buildings mapped, for the first time in detail, on the 1847 plan. Although not a new building, a telling factor in this respect is the purchase by the Bank of Ireland of the old parliament building, a development that led to the establishment of Dame Street as the new financial hub (see **30**). With the rise of the joint-stock bank after 1820, the Royal Bank of Ireland, the Provincial Bank of Ireland and the Newcomen and Latouche Banks added to the existing air of prosperity in this part of the city.[40] The Latouche Bank no longer survives but the other three bank buildings speak volumes of the capitalistic supremacy of these institutions in the nineteenth century, a characteristic exemplified in the magnificent architecture on this part of Dame Street. Another building of note was Commercial Buildings, which occupied

the stretch between Fownes Street and Anglesea Street and was the centre of gravity of the mercantile trade in Dublin for much of the nineteenth century.[41] However, nowhere on the street was affluence better represented than in Thomas Cooley's Royal Exchange (City Hall) on Cork Hill (see **31**). This cluster of financial institutions along Dame Street represents wealth and power in the early nineteenth-century city.

With surplus capital in the hands of the mercantile classes, the new railway technology presented an ideal opportunity for investment. After a tentative start and inspired by the example of their British counterparts, Irish businessmen eventually began to invest money in

Fig. 3: Carlisle Bridge and Sackville Street, *c.* 1850 (private collection).

railways.[42] By 1847 Dublin already had four rail termini, each one an emphatic statement of prosperity for the private company that it represented. The Midland Great Western, and the Great Southern and Western termini, located in the north-west and west of the city respectively, are easily the most impressive specimens of railway architecture (see **6**, **18**, **23**, **44**). Excess wealth also ensured that the

INTRODUCTION

eighteenth-century consumer market for luxury goods was sustained into the nineteenth century and that traditional shopping districts such as Grafton Street and its immediate environs thrived. Although the 1847 plan does not identify specific shops, this feature of the city's economy is nevertheless represented in the built fabric of the traditional shopping streets. Such economic buoyancy even filtered down to street level with the growth and regulation of the market place influencing the topography north and south of the Liffey.[43] While the older city markets such as the Smithfield cattle and hay market, the Ormond Street market, and Newmarket in the Liberties had been in place since before Rocque's period, others such as the egg and poultry market and fruit market at Petticoat Lane north of Little Mary Street, and the two vegetable markets and fish market south of the same street, were new additions and gave character and personality to what became the north city market district in the nineteenth century (see **9**). The Leinster meat market in D'Olier Street and the Northumberland Market in Abbey Street were also nineteenth-century additions, appearing, for the first time, on the 1847 map.[44]

One of the most prominent features of the city's topographical development during the nineteenth century was investment in church building, not least that of Roman Catholic chapels in the period after 1829. The map shows the city divided by parish and ward. Each parish represented the Established Church and was named after the saint to which its church was dedicated. South of the Liffey, both within and without the old medieval core, the two ancient cathedrals of Christ Church and St Patrick's dominate the ecclesiastical landscape of the nineteenth-century city. Christ Church is shown in all its glory as the centrepiece of the Wide Streets Commissioners' improvements in Christchurch Place (see **36**). Farther south St Patrick's stands adjacent to the slums of Goodman's Lane and Walker's Alley, removed and replaced in the 1860s by St Patrick's Park as part of Benjamin Lee Guinness's rejuvenation scheme (see **35**). Across the river on Marlborough Street, the Pro-Cathedral stands in tribute to Archbishop Troy of Dublin who was responsible for raising funds for its erection in 1814–25 (see **15**).[45] From an architectural perspective, other notable Church of Ireland parish churches in 1847 included St George's, Hardwicke Place, St Catherine's, Thomas Street (see **12**, **39**), and of course the Chapel Royal in Dublin Castle designed by Francis Johnston.

Catholic church architecture is noteworthy during this period as it demonstrates an institution recovering from the restrictive shackles of the penal laws. This is exemplified in a number of church buildings, including St Michan's in Halston Street whose front entrance was moved after 1829 to a more prominent site than the previous low-key entrance on Anne Street North (see **8**).[46] The progressive tendency of the Catholic church during this period of reform is also evident in the large and impressive St Andrew's on Westland Row. As the parish church of none other than Daniel O'Connell, the great champion of Catholic emancipation, it was fitting that this church should, in architecture and grandeur, reflect the enhanced status of the Catholic church in Ireland. A previous parish church had been in progress but was halted in favour of the larger and more fitting St Andrew's that opened in 1833–4 (see **23**).[47] Other church buildings such as John's Lane and the Carmelite church on Whitefriar Street are representative of an institution on the rise (see **32**).

The district surrounding Whitefriar Street had been a Methodist stronghold in the eighteenth century and the Methodist connection was still strong in 1847. North of the Carmelite church was Whitefriars Hall, occupying the site of the eighteenth-century meeting house once used by the Methodist Missionary Society (see **32**).[48] West of the hall the Methodist Orphan School House and Alms House remained in 1847. The map shows a scattering of Methodist chapels spread about the city as far apart as Cork Street and Bride Street in the south-west, to Hardwick Place in the north-east, and including Abbey Street, Blackhall Place and St Stephen's Green in the centre, north and south of the Liffey. A strong Presbyterian presence is shown in Great Strand Street and the district around Upper Ormond Quay where meeting houses and Scots' churches are depicted (see **10**). Quaker communities are also shown around St Stephen's Green east and in Cork Street.

The great bastion of higher education in Dublin, Trinity College, stands at the heart of the modern east-orientated capital created by the Wide Streets Commissioners (see **28**, **30**). Its magnificent eighteenth-century architecture funded by generous parliamentary grants and surrounded by extensive parks and gardens makes for one of the most aesthetically pleasing sites in the city, both in 1847 and today.[49] The other great institute of higher education in the city in 1847 was the Royal College of Surgeons on St Stephen's Green West, designed

INTRODUCTION

by Edward Parke in 1805 (see **26**).[50] The map precedes by seven years the founding of the Catholic University, spearheaded by Cardinals Cullen and Newman. The Royal College of Physicians on Kildare Street was also a later addition to the city's educational landscape, not being founded until 1862.[51] In some cases schools of medicine were attached to hospitals, as was St Peter's Hospital and the Dublin School of Medicine and Surgery in Peter Street (see **32**), and the School of Pharmacy at the Apothecaries' Hall in Mary Street (see **10**). One of the more prestigious institutions for the education of young boys was the Blue Coat Hospital on Blackhall Place established in 1670 (see **2**). On Sir John Rogerson's Quay in the eastern maritime quarter the Hibernian Marine School established by parliamentary grant in 1775 specialised more in technical education, providing maintenance and apprenticeships for the children of seamen (see **21**).[52]

The education of children was closely tied with religion, and the church and school house were often attached. In 1835 the newly-formed Commissioners for National Education established a new complex of model schools in Marlborough Street incorporating Tyrone House, the former home of Marcus Beresford. The complex is the present site of the Department of Education (see **15**) and included a male and female and infant model school, and a teacher training college, inspired no doubt by the training college of the Kildare Place Society. Once established in Marlborough Street, the commissioners rolled out a system of national model schools.[53] By 1847 all of the parishes within the municipal boundary of Dublin had a boys' and girls' national school. Not included on the map but apparent in other sources were the many private schools of music, language and art, in addition to the numerous learned societies and academies, none more so than the Royal Irish Academy on Grafton Street opposite the Provost's House (see **28**).[54]

Improvements in transport and mobility led to unprecedented demographic growth, particularly in the years leading to the famine, the population growing from 178,603 in 1821 to 258,369 by 1851.[55] With such a dramatic increase it is hardly surprising that social conditions declined as they did and the great influx of poor was made all the more apparent by the mass exodus of the wealthy in the aftermath of the Act of Union. The story is well-documented: the great town houses of the rich became the tenements of the poor and unemployment, poverty, disease and crime became pressing issues for the government and municipal authorities. The government response to

these social issues, more than anything else, gives nineteenth-century Dublin its dour institutional character with prisons, hospitals, workhouses and barracks featuring prominently in the north and south-west inner city. This aspect comes to the fore in the 1847 town plan (see **1**, **3**, **4**, **8**, **38**, **39**, **42**, **43**).

With the Vartry water scheme a long way off in 1862, the city had an inadequate supply, with many parts such as Phibsborough and Stoneybatter still dependent on wells sunk in the gardens of properties. In many parts of the Liberties such as The Coombe, Newmarket, Meath Street, Ward's Hill and Brabazon Row, the water pipes, as depicted on the map, were still made of wood (see **37**).[56] Notwithstanding this, the south-west Liberties district had an abundant supply of water owing to the presence of the Rivers Poddle and Camac. On a city-wide level, however, water supply was less than adequate. This was particularly so in the back lanes and alleys, such as Verschoyle Court in the Mount Street district where one fountain supplied ninety-eight separate properties (see **22**). A major defect in the system was that the city's water supply in 1840 was under the control of two authorities: the paving commissioners had control of the fountains and possessed the power to open the streets if necessary, while the actual supply of water was under the control of the corporation which had no authority to open the streets for repairs.[57] Insufficient water supply, coupled with poor sewerage and drainage facilities, led inevitably to the spread of disease and nowhere was this more apparent than in the squalid tenement conditions where as many as ten families often occupied one house. The great political reform of the 1830s and 1840s brought the issue of public health in towns under the microscope and resulted in the passing of important legislation in 1840 and 1848, which helped to address the problems of insanitary living conditions.[58] In fact a recommendation of the commissioners appointed to inquire into the health of towns in 1840 was that drains, sewers and supply conduits should be inserted on the five-foot plans.[59]

Overcrowded and insanitary living conditions led to sickness and disease and the first half of the nineteenth century saw a multitude of hospitals open their doors to the poor and destitute of Dublin. The majority of these institutions began as philanthropic endeavours since charity and philanthropy were the only means of tackling such prevailing social evils. The Charitable Infirmary (see **10**) had been established early in the eighteenth century, but acquired a larger

INTRODUCTION

better-fitted premises in Jervis Street in 1803.[60] The same year saw the Hardwicke Fever Hospital (see **3**) open and a few years later the Cork Fever Hospital (see **38**) was established. In 1811 and 1817 the Richmond Surgical and the Whitworth Hospitals were founded (see **3**), which along with the Hardwicke made up the House of Industry Hospitals on Brunswick Street North.[61] With the majority of poor females giving birth in the home, such deplorable living conditions led to high infant mortality and a lying-in hospital dedicated to impoverished women was identified as an urgent requirement. In 1826 the Coombe Lying-in Hospital (see **37**) was established for the poor of the Liberties and in 1835 the Western Lying-in Hospital (see **2**) for the western parishes of St Paul's and St Michan's. In 1822 the new Meath Hospital (see **34**) was built and in 1834 St Vincent's Hospital on St Stephen's Green (see **26**) was established by the Religious Sisters of Charity.[62] The majority of these institutions, along with many of their older eighteenth-century counterparts, were funded by charitable and philanthropic means.

Dublin in 1847 was a city of both wealth and poverty. While many of its more elaborate public buildings were erected in the mid to late eighteenth century, the impressive banking architecture on Dame Street and the city's four majestic railway termini attest to the new-found wealth of the post-Union city, where a rising commercial elite gradually eclipsed the last remnants of a powerful landed class. This new wealth was embodied by the merchants, bankers and professional classes and, as wealth afforded the luxury of leisure, the nineteenth-century city with its numerous clubs, music halls, theatres and libraries provided ample opportunity for the entertainment of its *nouveaux riches*. Private gentlemen's clubs such as the Kildare Street Club, St Stephen's Green Club and Hibernian United Service Club — the former two with their racket courts to the rear — provided a home from home for the wealthy gentlemen of the city and its hinterlands (see **26**, **27**). Leisure, however, was not the sole reserve of the privileged and some establishments catered for the middling and less affluent members of society. Music halls are a good example and the Music Hall on Abbey Street Lower (see **14**) and Astley's Royal Amphitheatre of Horsemanship in Peter Street (see **32**) catered for the great and the good in Dublin society, as did the Theatre Royal in Hawkins Street (see **29**).[63]

With so many beautiful public squares and gardens, the promenade was a favourite activity of the wealthy in summer afternoons and evenings. In addition to the residential squares (see **11**, **12**, **24**, **25**, **26**), so too the harbour at Broadstone and the City Basin provided pleasing surroundings for taking a leisurely waterside stroll (see **6**, **41**). The gardens at Trinity College and Portobello were also popular locations for taking the air; by 1850 the Portobello Gardens were known as the Palace of Cheap Amusements (see **28**, **33**).[64] While the architecture of capitalism affirms a prosperous side to the nineteenth-century city, by the same token the numerous almshouses, orphanages, hospitals and asylums attest to its poverty. Bathing houses such as the Royal Baths at Westland Row (see **23**) and Northumberland Baths at Abbey Street Lower (see **14**) gave entertainment to the less privileged classes, while even the most persecuted souls sought out leisure (or perhaps pleasure) in the back-alley ball courts, brothels and taverns located in the vicinity of the city's prisons and barracks (see **1**, **8**, **19**, **35**, **40**, **43**).

CONCLUSION

Considering the immense topographical change that occurred in the city of Dublin between 1756 and 1847,[65] the Ordnance Survey large-scale plan was both timely and important. Besides the physical transformation caused by such important engineering schemes as the Royal Canal extension to Broadstone and the eastward extension of the port, so too were the various improvement schemes of the Wide Streets Commissioners, along with new public buildings such as the Custom House, Four Courts and General Post Office, all mapped, for the first time, in astonishing detail. The squares and gardens of the Georgian city, absent — with the exception of St Stephen's Green — from Rocque's map, are also captured and depicted in astounding beauty by the embellishers back in Phoenix Park headquarters. The 1830s and 1840s was the great period of railway technology and the new railway architecture and ancillary developments are conspicuous in their appearance, stamped as they were over the old city template. In short, the Ordnance Survey 1847 town plan for Dublin city represents a unique, fascinating and immensely detailed visual record of Ireland's capital, as the Great Famine took hold.

INTRODUCTION

[1] James M'Glashan, *Dublin and its environs* (Dublin, 1850), pp 1–2.

[2] OS town plans, 1:1056, Dublin, 1847.

[3] J.H. Andrews, *A paper landscape: the Ordnance Survey in nineteenth-century Ireland* (Oxford, 2002), pp 14–15.

[4] Andrews, *A paper landscape*, pp 31–2.

[5] By 1840 Lieutenant Thomas Aiskew Larcom had progressed to the rank of captain and was eventually knighted in 1860.

[6] Bridget Hourican and James Quinn, 'Sir Thomas Aiskew Larcom', in *Dictionary of Irish biography* (Cambridge, 2009).

[7] Charles Close, *The early years of the Ordnance Survey* (Newton Abbot, 1969), pp 119–32.

[8] Ibid., p. 119.

[9] Ibid., p. 126.

[10] Captain Henry Tucker went on to head operations in the Phoenix Park in 1853–4, see Andrews, *A paper landscape*, p. 331.

[11] OS progress reports 1836–7, OS 1/13 (NAI); OS fair plans, Dublin, OS 105 E (NAI).

[12] OS letter register, letters 7132, 31 Dec. 1836 and 8056, Aug. 1838, OS 2/16 (NAI).

[13] OS letter register, letter 6744, 28 Apr. 1836, OS 2/14 (NAI).

[14] OS field books, Dublin city, OS 58 E (NAI).

[15] OS progress report, October 1836, OS 1/13 (NAI).

[16] A degree of uncertainty still surrounds the evolution of the Dublin town plans. OS 139 in the NAI is an incomplete series of maps covering the south-west district of Dublin city from Cork Street north as far as Usher's Quay, in addition to the Custom House and Sir John Rogerson's Quay in the port district. Although drafted at a scale of 1:1056, these maps record far greater detail than appears on the 1:1056 manuscript and printed plans of 1843 and 1847. The exact purpose of these maps is difficult to ascertain and it remains unclear as to why such detail was recorded, and if indeed the series was ever completed to cover the entire city.

[17] Andrews, *A paper landscape*, p. 185.

[18] The term 'ornamentation' in Ordnance Survey usage refers to land cover, for example trees, grass and house-fillings, and does not refer to non-topographical decoration such as shellwork, cherubs and acanthus leaves.

[19] OS 1837 fair plans, OS 105 E 294/299/300 (NAI); OS town plans, 1:1056, Dublin, manuscript 1843 (NAI).

[20] OS town plans, 1:1056, Dublin, manuscript, OS 140, 1843, sheet 9 (NAI).

[21] OS town plans, 1:1056, Dublin, manuscript, OS 140, 1843 (NAI), and OS town plans, 1:1056, Dublin, 1847.

[22] OS field books, Dublin city, OS 58 E (NAI).

[23] Ibid.

[24] OS town plans, 1:1056, Dublin, manuscript 1843, sheet 33, OS 140 (NAI), OS town plans, 1:1056, Dublin, 1847, sheet 28; OS field books, Dublin city, OS 58 E (NAI).

[25] *Illustrated London News,* iv, no. 90 (20 Jan. 1844), p. 37.

[26] Close, *The early years of the Ordnance Survey*, pp 111–12.

[27] Although it had its origins in discussions surrounding the possible closure of Mountjoy House, the dispute came to the fore when Larcom refused to send Irish records to Southampton as instructed by Colby. Colby responded by dismissing Larcom from the Survey. See Andrews, *A paper landscape*, pp 182, 185, 198–202.

[28] Ibid., pp 201, 211.

[29] OS letter register, OS 2/20 (314), 2 Feb. 1847 (NAI).

[30] Colby had retired from the Ordnance Survey in April 1847.

[31] OS letter register, OS 2/20 (315), 18 May 1847 (NAI).

[32] OS letter register, OS 2/20 (378), 4 Feb. 1848 (NAI).

[33] OS letter register, OS 2/20 (374–5), 21, 24 June 1848 (NAI).

[34] OS letter register, OS 2/20 (1,154), 14 Dec. 1853 (NAI).

[35] Rob Goodbody, *Dublin, part III, 1756 to 1847* (Irish Historic Towns Atlas, no. 26, Dublin, 2014); *General reports of the census of Ireland, 1851.*

[36] Goodbody, *Dublin part III, 1756 to 1847*; Christine Casey, *Dublin: the city within the Grand and Royal Canals and the Circular Road with the Phoenix Park* (London and New Haven, 2005), pp 46, 417, 420.

INTRODUCTION

[37] H.A. Gilligan, *A history of the port of Dublin* (Dublin, 1988), p. 132.

[38] OS town plans, 1:1056, Dublin, 1847, sheets 16, 17.

[39] Francis Cullen, 'Local government and the management of urban space: a comparative study of Belfast and Dublin, 1830–1922', Ph.D., NUI Maynooth (2005), pp 55–60.

[40] J.W. Gilbart, *The history of banking in Ireland* (London, 1836), pp 60–61.

[41] William Curry, *The picture of Dublin or stranger's guide to the Irish metropolis* (Dublin, 1835), p. 93.

[42] Joseph Lee, 'The provision of capital for early Irish railways, 1830–53', in *Irish Historical Studies,* xvi (1968), pp 34–5.

[43] Curry, *The picture of Dublin*, p. 9.

[44] OS town plans, 1:1056, Dublin, 1847.

[45] Casey, *Dublin*, p. 126.

[46] Peter Pearson, *The heart of Dublin: resurgence of an historic city* (Dublin, 2000), p. 346.

[47] Casey, *Dublin*, pp 451–2.

[48] J.J. M'Gregor, *New picture of Dublin: comprehending a history of the city, an accurate account of its various establishments and institutions, and a correct description of all the public edifices connected with them* (Dublin, 1821), p. 238; Steven Ffeary-Smyrl. 'Theatres of worship: dissenting meeting houses in Dublin, 1650–1750', in Kevin Herlihy (ed.), *The Irish dissenting tradition 1650–1750* (Dublin, 1995), pp 61–2.

[49] John Warburton, James Whitelaw and Robert Walsh, *History of the city of Dublin, from the earliest accounts to the present time, volume 1* (London, 1818), p. 657.

[50] Casey, *Dublin*, p. 484.

[51] S.M. Parkes, 'Higher education, 1793–1908', in W.E. Vaughan (ed.), *A new history of Ireland VI: Ireland under the Union II 1870–1921* (Oxford, 1996), pp 552–3.

[52] Warburton, Whitelaw and Walsh, *History of the city of Dublin*, pp 614, 657.

[53] Judith Harford, 'Ireland', in Tom O'Donoghue and Clive Whitehead (eds), *Teacher education in the English-speaking world: past, present and future* (Dublin, 2008), p. 76.

[54] See various issues of *Saunders Newsletter* throughout the 1840s.

[55] W.E. Vaughan and A.J. Fitzpatrick (eds), *Irish historical statistics: population 1821–1971* (Dublin, 1978), p. 5.

[56] OS 1847 Dublin 1:1056, sheets 20, 26. In 1802 Dublin Corporation began replacing the old wooden water pipes with metal pipes and in 1809 imposed a new 'metal main tax' upon the citizens to defray the expense. As the earl of Meath's liberty fell outside the jurisdiction of the corporation many of the water pipes in this part of the city, as late as 1847, were still made of wood. See Warburton, Whitelaw and Walsh, *History of the city of Dublin*, pp 1069–74.

[57] *Report from the select committee on the health of towns; together with the minutes of evidence taken before them, and an appendix, and index*, H.C. 1840 (384), xi, evidence of H. Maunsell, 29 May 1840, p. 199.

[58] Municipal Corporations (Ireland) Act, 1840 (3 & 4 Vict., c. 108); Public Health Act, 1848 (11 & 12 Vict., c. 63).

[59] OS letter register (9), OS 2/20 (NAI), 4 May 1846.

[60] This institution was originally founded in a small house in Cook Street in 1721 before moving, by way of King's Inns Quay, to its final location, the site of the former Charlemont House, on Jervis Street. Here, in 1803, a new house was built. See Goodbody, *Dublin, part III, 1756 to 1847*, p. 88; McGregor, *New picture of Dublin*, p. 287.

[61] Goodbody, *Dublin, part III, 1756 to 1847*, pp 49, 89.

[62] Ibid., pp 88–90; Casey, *Dublin*, p. 660; Curry, *The picture of Dublin*, p. 300.

[63] Linde Lunney, 'Philip Astley', in *Dictionary of Irish Biography* (Cambridge, 2009).

[64] *Freeman's Journal,* 21 Aug. 1855.

[65] For a comprehensive study of Dublin's changing topography during this period, see Goodbody, *Dublin, part III, 1756 to 1847.*

INTRODUCTION

PART II: Map extracts and commentaries

The original printed Ordnance Survey town plans of Dublin (1847) used for the following extracts are in the National Library of Ireland. See the editorial note on p. xi for further details.

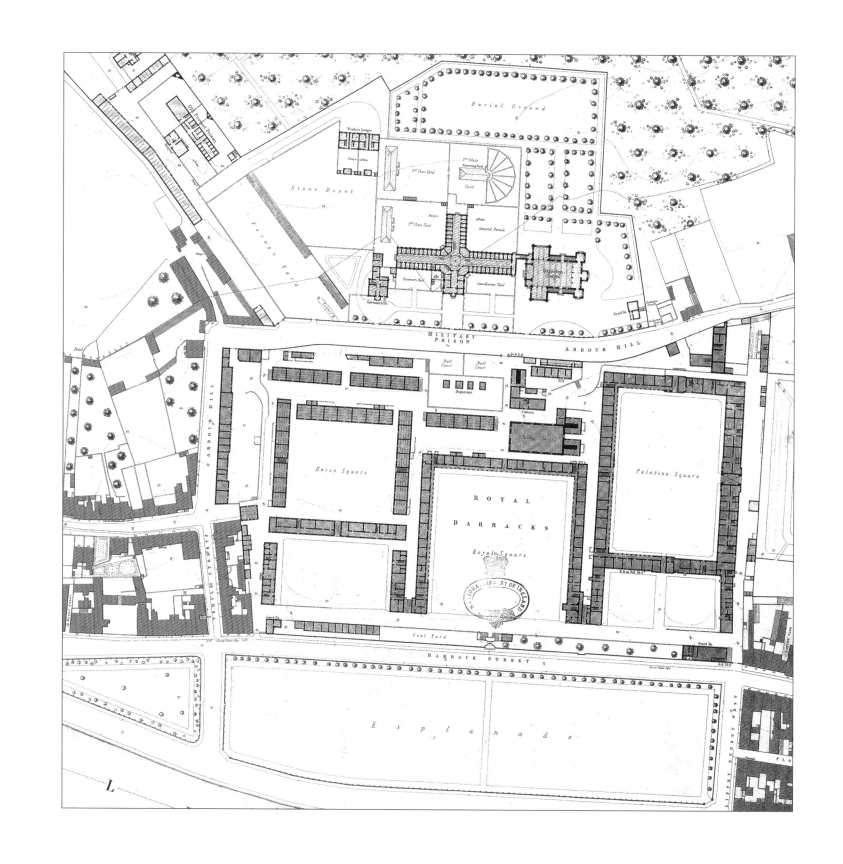

In 1847 the Royal Barracks, built in 1708, stood at the centre of the British military operation in Ireland. Its location on the western edge of the city assumed additional strategic importance with the arrival of the railway after 1840. Close proximity to the Kingsbridge and Broadstone termini made possible the rapid dispatch of troops in times of emergency. In 1847 most of the original eighteenth-century complex remained intact, yet some alterations are apparent on close examination of the map. The three squares presenting onto the Liffey are relatively unchanged from their appearance on John Rocque's map of 1756, which depicts them from west to east as Horse Square, Royal Square and Little Square (Fig. 4, right). By the 1790s Horse Square had been completely rebuilt and renamed Cavalry Square, yet along with the former Little Square, both are unnamed on the 1847 map. During this rebuilding stage a new Horse Square was added directly north of Cavalry Square. Located north of the former Little Square is the impressively large Palatine Square, fully closed in by 1847 as opposed to its three-sided appearance in 1756. Another mid-nineteenth-century remnant of the eighteenth-century ensemble was the riding school situated directly north of Royal Square. Originally built as a chapel, it was soon after converted to the riding school with some modifications as shown on the 1847 plan.

New buildings, including a canteen, magazines and two ball courts for the recreation of the soldiers, are depicted north of Horse and Royal Squares in the extract. By comparing this plan with Rocque's map of 1756, it can be seen how the street known as Arbour Hill was redirected to accommodate the construction of the new Horse Square and then separated the main barrack buildings from the military prison and garrison chapel via a connecting tunnel. The plan also shows evidence of the classification of military prisoners with three separate yards for 1st, 2nd and 3rd class prisoners. This distinction is further marked by the presence of an exercising shed in the 1st class yard, as opposed to work sheds for prisoners of 2nd and 3rd class status. According to a parliamentary return of 1847, the barrack water supply was derived from a pond located within the grounds and connected to the Vice Regal Lodge in the nearby Phoenix Park. While such a pond does not appear on the Ordnance Survey plan within the barrack grounds, a small pond shown just west of the barracks may well be the one in question. A number of pumps and a well are also depicted within the grounds of the military prison.

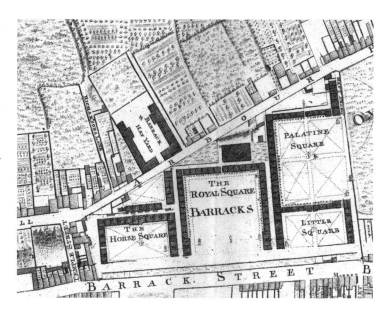

Fig. 4: Royal Barracks, extract from John Rocque's *Exact survey*, 1756 (Map Library, TCD).

In the immediate vicinity of the barracks a small business community benefited from the military presence. Of the seven occupied houses on Liffey Street West, all were private businesses. These included three shoemakers, a carpenter, a glazier, a dressmaker, a bonnet maker, and Peter Molloy's vintners and billiard room at no. 7 and also no. 10 on Pembroke Quay. From a social perspective the most notorious aspect of the barracks was the link between soldiers and prostitution. In the *United Service Journal* in 1837 the buildings on Barrack Street were described as 'a line of brothels and low public houses ... and filled with the most abandoned crew of rogues and prostitutes which even all Dublin ... can produce'. These buildings are visible on Rocque's map and remained until 1836 when they were purchased by the Wide Streets Commissioners and removed to make way for the handsome esplanade fronting the barracks onto the quay. Known today as the Croppy Acre, the esplanade serves as a memorial to the men who died in the 1798 rebellion.

1. ROYAL BARRACKS

The Blue Coat Hospital was originally established in 1670, its principal objective being to provide education and care for the sons of freemen of the city. Originally located in Queen Street, the school removed to a site close to Oxmantown Green in 1773. The new building, designed by Thomas Ivory, is shown on the western side of Blackhall Place perpendicular to Blackhall Street (Fig. 5, below). The front elevation is of Portland stone and measures 300 feet in width. Separating the main building from Blackhall Place is a spacious court enclosed by iron railings. Two Palladian walls lead from the main building towards a north and south wing. The north wing housed a chapel, while the south functioned as a schoolroom. To the rear was a section containing dormitories, a dining hall and an infirmary. Beyond the garden a large bowling green provided for the exercise of the young boys. The location of the Pipe Water Stores south of the Blue Coat Hospital at 15 Barrack Street was somewhat ironic, since prior to the arrival of the Vartry water in 1862 the northwest part of the city had the poorest supply of piped water owing to its location on high ground (see **5**).

The district between the Blue Coat Hospital and Smithfield contained a number of religious institutions of different denominations. South-east of the Established Church Blue Coat Hospital, on the corner of Blackhall Place and Hendrick Place, stood the Methodist chapel dating from 1770. This chapel had the distinction of being the first Methodist chapel built on the north side of the city. The main determining factor in its location was proximity to the Royal Barracks (see **1**) housing over 1,500 men and their families. Nearby at Blackhall Parade was St Paul's Church of Ireland dating from 1824. In 1835 St Paul's was described as a 'neat edifice with a small spire' and a 'tolerable and spacious' churchyard. The Royal Barracks was also a determining factor in this church's location and the churchyard immediately south of the main building was used mostly to inter the bodies of military men. Farther south on Arran Quay is St Paul's Catholic Chapel, designed by Patrick Byrne in 1835 and still in use today. Poverty was a prevailing issue for concerned authorities in the parish of St Paul's and the neighbouring parish of St Michan's. In 1835 the Western Lying-in Hospital at 24 Arran Quay opened its doors to the poor and needy females of these and other nearby parishes.

The centre of gravity of this district was of course Smithfield. This open market space was dominated to the east by the Jameson whiskey distillery on Bow Street. At the northern end of Smithfield was the convict depot, formerly the Smithfield Penitentiary opened in 1801 to cater for offenders under the age of fifteen awaiting transportation. The idea was to reform the young offenders through a system of training. The establishment of the Smithfield Penitentiary was a pioneering move towards improving the conditions of children within the prison system. In 1844 it was converted to a convict depot to relieve pressure on the overcrowded Kilmainham Gaol (see **45**). The number of weighing houses in the district is a clue to the area's primary function as a market place. Two of these are shown in Hay Market, two at the south end of Smithfield and two at the north end, while another was located north of Carter Lane. Also of note is the brewery of Andrew Thunder at 14 and 15 Church Street New. Thunder sold the brewery in 1851 and moved to Bendigo outside Melbourne, Australia. There he established another brewery, which subsequently gave its name to the present Thunder Street in that town.

Fig. 5: Blue Coat Hospital, 1798, from James Malton, *A picturesque and descriptive view of the city of Dublin* (London, 1792–9).

2. BLUE COAT HOSPITAL AND SMITHFIELD

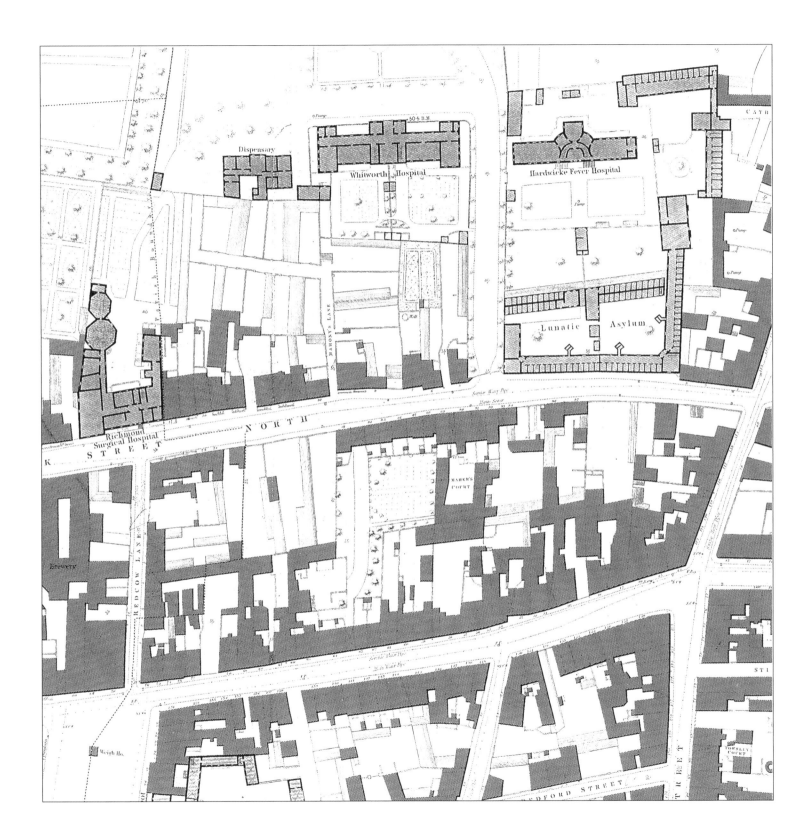

The district north of Brunswick Street North was one of two hospital districts in nineteenth-century Dublin. The other was located in the south-west part of the city and included Swift's, Dr Steevens and the Royal Hospital (see **43**). The House of Industry hospitals on Brunswick Street North incorporated the Hardwicke Fever Hospital (1803), Richmond Surgical Hospital (1811) and the Whitworth Hospital (1814). The Richmond Surgical Hospital was the only one directly visible from Brunswick Street North. The Hardwicke was to the rear of the lunatic asylum of the same name, which presented directly onto the main street. Access to the hospital appears to have been gained through a gateway on Brunswick Street North via a tree-lined avenue to a second east gateway leading to the front entrance. The same avenue may also have provided access to the asylum. The two-storey, 144-bed Hardwicke Hospital was divided into four wards, two for male and two for female patients, with a separate ward on each floor for convalescing patients. The attached asylum contained a combination of cells and wards to be used according to the patient's mental state. In 1835 the majority of the resident patients were deemed to be 'harmless and incurable'; what were termed 'idiots and epileptic patients' were also detained in the cells attached to the wards.

Located immediately west of the Hardwicke Fever Hospital, on the opposite side of the tree-lined avenue, was the Whitworth Hospital for the chronically ill, named after the lord lieutenant of the time. The hospital was originally established to care for inmates of the House of Industry, but also treated paupers from all parts of the city in need of medical attention. The building was of plain calp stone with two storeys over basement and a north-facing front seventeen bays across. The map shows an advanced central block, which was crowned with a pediment above the front entrance. Inside, a large entrance hall led directly into the physician's room flanked on either side by a staircase. Above this room a dormitory and other apartments were used by the matron and staff. Patients' wards were located at the east and west extremities of the building. The hospital could accommodate about eighty patients in eight ten-bed wards, four located on each floor.

The Richmond Surgical Hospital shown on the 1847 map no longer exists, having been demolished to make way for a new Richmond Hospital in the 1890s. This later nineteenth-century building survives and serves as a courthouse today. The hospital building named on the 1847 map had previously been a Dominican convent, but was renovated in 1810 to suit its new medical function. Cramped accommodation was remodelled and a new wing added to provide clean and comfortable facilities for the patients. In addition to the necessary operating theatre, the hospital had a library and museum funded by the surgeons and medical students. The hospital opened on 4 June 1811 and in its first six months admitted 578 patients. While priority was given to inmates of the House of Industry in need of hospital treatment, where possible other cases of destitution were considered. Immediately north-east of the hospital on the map was the Richmond Dispensary, which tended to the needs of the sick in the poorer parishes of the north-western city. A physician and surgeon attended daily and even visited the homes of those unable to travel.

3. NORTH CITY HOSPITAL QUARTER

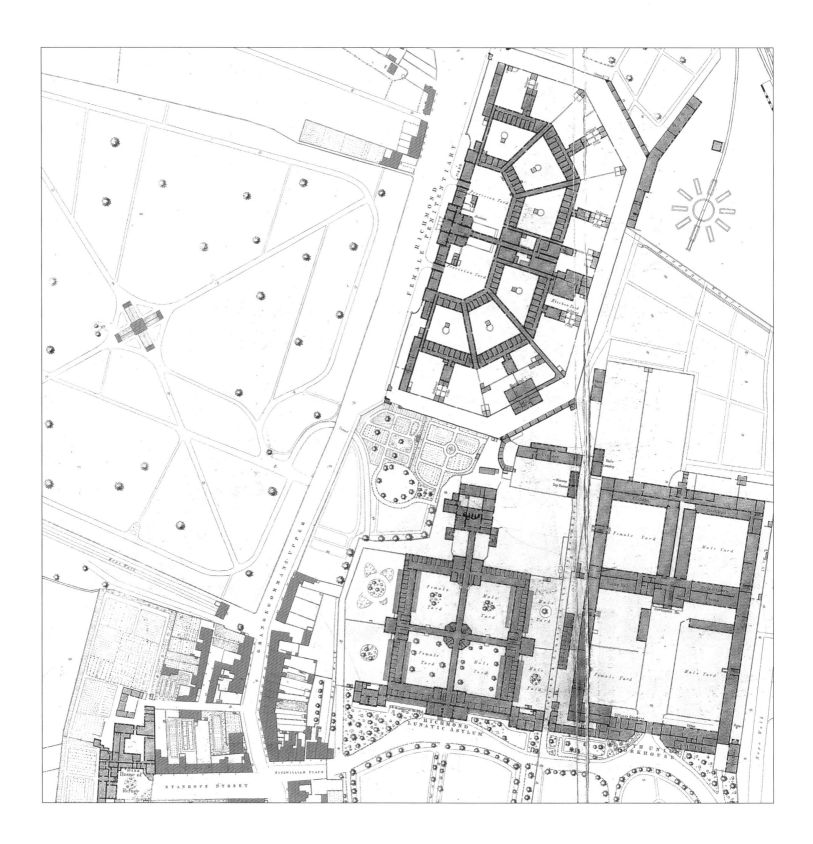

The Grangegorman district in the north-western part of the city underwent dramatic transformation during the half century from 1770 to 1820. The erection of a series of institutional buildings designed to intimidate and incarcerate changed irreversibly the character of this once rural suburb. The establishment of the House of Industry in 1772 was the first step in this process, setting the tone for the future development of the district. In 1791 the House of Industry was moved to a new building and the original premises was demolished to make way for the Richmond Lunatic Asylum. Over the coming decades the House of Industry gave rise to a number of surrounding institutional buildings, including the Whitworth and Hardwicke Fever Hospitals, and with the establishment of the Poor Law in 1838 it became the workhouse of the North Dublin Union.

The segregation of the sexes was implemented here as in all union workhouses, whether they were newly built or an adapted premises; the disposition of rooms in Francis Johnston's building, as depicted on the Ordnance Survey map, reflects the tight control that underpinned the new system (for other works by Johnston see 7, 13, 14, 19, 30, 31, 42, 43). Four open-air courtyards within the main quadrangle provided for the exercise of male and female inmates, males to the east side and females to the west. The inmates of the North Dublin Union were unusually well looked after in terms of religious provision, having both a Catholic and a Protestant chapel on site. The large dining hall offered at least limited opportunities for both sexes to mix. Together with the governor's house, officers' quarters, girls' laundry, straw house and stables, these apartments comprised about half of the entire complex, the remaining space being utilised for cramped accommodation of the inmates. The neighbouring Richmond Lunatic Asylum, also designed by Johnston, was of a less austere composition. Once again the complex was built around four main courtyards set out for male and female patients in a similar manner to the workhouse, with an octagonal centrepiece housing privies. Two further yards, each for male and female patients, were located immediately east of the main quadrangle. Compared to the grim utilitarian nature of the adjacent workhouse, the asylum had a more aesthetically pleasing appearance with shrubbery and walkways depicted within the grounds of the complex.

Probably the most foreboding building in the entire city during this period was the Richmond Female Penitentiary. In this sober structure clear emphasis was given to the purpose and objective of the building, and its appearance on the map draws the eye immediately to the north-western suburb of Grangegorman. Another example of Johnston's work, the female penitentiary represented the epitome of early nineteenth-century penal architecture. The massive seventeen-bay, three-storey, unrelenting façade advancing right to the edge of the street was designed with one effect in mind: to intimidate. No gravel walkways or shrubbery greet the incoming prisoner, just cold grey calp. The overall plan was radial in layout, the classic panopticon, allowing a very small staff to keep the entire complex under perpetual surveillance, with prisoners confined to individual cells that they might reflect on their crimes and be more amenable to reform. Within the main entrance two provision yards stood on either side of the dividing corridor. Six open courtyards are also visible on the map, each containing a privy for the use of the inmates. A bathing house, labelled on the 1843 manuscript map but not on the later 1847 printed version, was situated in the block south of the main entrance. Farther to the rear of the complex were the solitary cells, hospital, dining room, kitchen and laundry. Located immediately south of the main complex were the nursery day rooms that presumably housed the infants of the female inmates. Only part of the front façade survives today, the scale of which gives some idea as to the brooding effect of this building in 1847.

4. NORTH DUBLIN UNION WORKHOUSE

The suburb of Phibsborough, with the Circular Road running through its village centre, was an interesting, yet underdeveloped, part of the city in 1847. Just north of the Broadstone district, it fell outside the bounds of John Rocque's map of the city in 1756. The laying out of the Circular Road in the 1780s attracted initial development in the area and over the next century Phibsborough was gradually drawn into the city as residential and engineering schemes obliterated the rural buffer zone that had kept it apart. Following the construction of the Royal Canal branch into Broadstone Harbour, housing development on both sides of Phibsborough Road increased with new streets such as Monck Place, Norton's Row and Phibsborough Avenue being laid out. The accompanying extract shows a well-maintained, heavily gardened district from Monck Place, north as far as Fassaugh Lane, and includes Phibsborough House, now gone, and Oak Lodge. Situated on high ground, Phibsborough and Prussia Street were the last parts of the city to receive piped water in the early part of the nineteenth century, hence the numerous private pumps and wells sunk in the gardens of many of the properties. This worked to the district's advantage when in 1862 it was the first part of the city to receive the new Vartry water. By 1847 the railway had also become a factor in the growth of this suburb, attracting further property development in the area, particularly later in the century with the laying out of Great Western Square, southwest of the R.C. chapel (St Peter's Church).

At the junction of the Circular Road and Phibsborough Road, the present Doyle's Corner, stood two turnpike gates, one on either side of the street with the Toll House shown on the south-west corner. East of Madras Place is Blacquiere Bridge, named after Sir John Blacquiere, a director of the Royal Canal Company. Farther west, St Peter's Church (Fig. 6, above), situated on the fork between the Circular Road and Cabragh Road, remains an important landmark in Phibsborough. The present church is of 1858 by the architects Weightman, Hadfield and Goldie of Sheffield. This is a substantial

Fig. 6: St Peter's Church, Phibsborough, 1825, by George Petrie, from G.N. Wright, *An historical guide to the city of Dublin* (London, 1825).

reworking of the original 1820s church depicted on the map and shown in the accompanying illustration by Petrie. This extract demonstrates well the extent of creativity employed by the draftsmen in the Phoenix Park headquarters when depicting the gardens of the city, since such minute detail was not captured in the surveyors' field books. Nevertheless, on completion of each draft, it was then taken back into the field to be examined on site before the engraving process commenced. The work on this particular sheet was undertaken by George McCoy. On the north side of the Circular Road opposite St Peter's Church is the site of the present Dalymount Park, the home of Bohemians Football Club. The vacant plot was acquired by the football club in 1901. The words 'Daly Mount' are recorded on the map for the short terrace of five houses north-east of St Peter's Church on the Circular Road, the longer terrace on the west side of Phibsborough Road and the cottages on the north side of Fassaugh Lane, now Connaught Street, just outside the extract.

5. THE PHIBSBOROUGH SUBURB

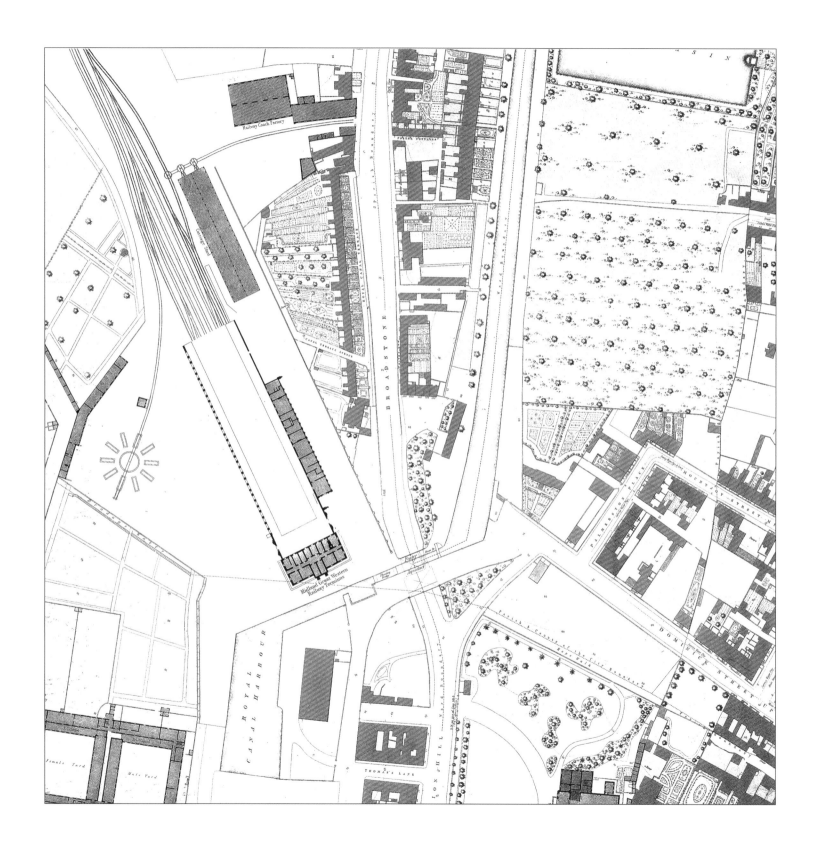

When John Rocque mapped Dublin in 1756, so unremarkable was the northern suburb of Grangegorman that he overwrote this featureless landscape with his title cartouche (Fig. 7, below right). By contrast, when the Ordnance Survey mapped the city over ninety years later in 1847, the same district had been transformed beyond recognition. Perhaps no other part of the city demonstrates such dramatic upheaval as this north city suburb, which by 1847 had become the most important transportation hub in the country with canal and railway converging on this once pastoral setting.

The decision by the Royal Canal Company directors in 1791 to build a branch line southwards from Cross Guns Bridge, linking up with a new harbour west of the road to Glasnevin, sealed the fate of the Grangegorman suburb. Close proximity to the north city markets was a deciding factor in locating the harbour. The original site had been planned for the intersection between Bolton Street and Dominick Street, but the less developed lands at Broadstone offered a cheaper alternative. Although less costly, the topography presented far greater engineering challenges since the canal had to be carried across the steep incline from Constitution Hill to Broadstone. The solution, the Foster Aqueduct, was erected by Miller & Ruddery in *c.* 1800 and dedicated to John Foster, the last speaker of the Irish House of Commons. Designed in the Egyptian Revival style, the bridge was one of the city's more noteworthy man-made landmarks. Via the aqueduct, the Royal Canal was carried across the Phibsborough Road and into the newly-built harbour.

When the Midland Great Western Railway company proposed its line to Galway, it also purchased the Royal Canal company's properties and built its terminus adjacent to the canal harbour at Broadstone. In clearing the site the old canal company's office at Royal Canal House was sacrificed for the main terminus building. Designed by John Skipton Mulvany in 1842, the Broadstone terminus is still striking in scale and style, with its Egyptian revival architecture heavily influenced by the nearby aqueduct. The 1847 map shows Robert

Mallet's floating bridge just west of the Foster Aqueduct. When not in use the bridge remained in a small purpose-built basin from where it could be floated into place as required. The bridge continued to serve its purpose until the 1870s when the canal and harbour were both filled in, having become redundant owing to the success of the railway. As a result the aqueduct became defunct and was redesigned as an approach roadway. It is both unfortunate and ironic that, having survived intact for over 150 years, this remarkable monument of nineteenth-century transportation engineering was viewed

Fig. 7: Title cartouche and extract showing Grangegorman, from John Rocque's *Exact survey*, 1756 (Map Library, TCD).

in 1951 as an impediment and was subsequently demolished. Mulvany's magnificent terminus building, notwithstanding the absence of the harbour, remains one of the most striking architectural sites in the city and its planned reopening as a commuter railway station is a welcome prospect for the Phibsborough district and the city as a whole.

6. BROADSTONE

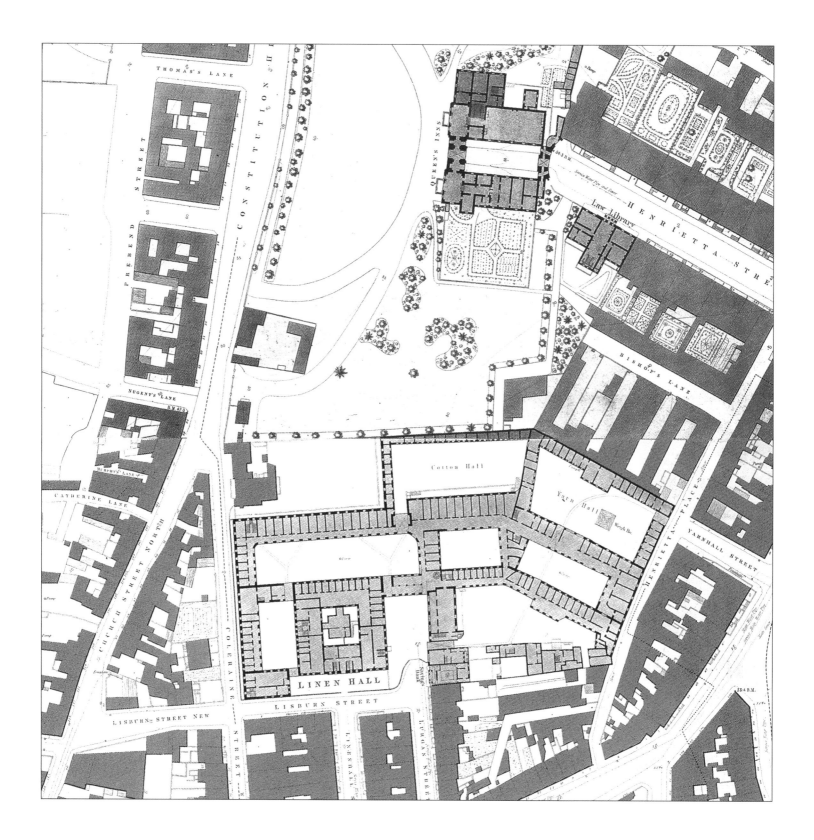

The Dublin Linen Hall, built in *c.* 1725, was still operating in 1847, despite a noticeable decline in commercial importance following the opening of the Belfast and Newry linen halls in 1783 and the subsequent dissolution of the Linen Board in 1828. The streets in the immediate vicinity, still in 1847, paid homage to the Ulster towns that lent their names to the various sizes of linen. Indeed Lurgan, Coleraine and Lisburn Streets remain today, while Derry Street, named on John Rocque's map of 1756, had disappeared by the 1780s to make way for Thomas Cooley's redevelopment of the three-acre site. In his new design Cooley retained the original hall by Thomas Burgh in the 1720s and part of the original building running along Coleraine Street (Fig. 8, right). The 1780s plan incorporated old with new and the northern part of Lurgan Street also disappeared to make way for the new buildings. The complex as it stood in 1847 consisted of six spacious courtyards surrounded by a series of storehouses linked by interconnecting galleries and piazzas. With the exception of the innermost yard, all the remaining yards communicated with one another via covered archways. Only two are named on the 1847 plan – the cotton hall to the rear of the complex and the adjacent yarn hall in the north-east corner. Three of the six yards were serviced by a single water pump located in each.

An important point in the history of the Dublin Linen Hall was the visit of King George IV to the establishment in 1821. To commemorate this historic event the linen merchants of the city erected a handsome marble statue of the king within the main building. The 1847 plan also shows a new branch of the Dublin Savings Bank immediately outside the main entrance in Lurgan Street. Administration of the institution was overseen by a chamberlain, who in turn reported to the Linen Board. Gatekeepers and watchmen were regularly employed along with a fire engine for emergencies, and sales finished at four o'clock each day since no light or fire was permitted inside the building. By 1847 new technologies in transportation and production had led to changes in the linen industry, with a steady decrease in the amounts of linen being sent from the country to Dublin. Yet the imposing scale of the complex in 1847, containing 557 storage apartments in addition to a coffee room and board room for the trustees, speaks of a prosperous institution despite the obvious decline in commercial activity.

Located immediately north of the linen hall, at the west end of Henrietta Street, was the King's Inns (referred to on the 1847 plan as Queen's Inns). Having vacated their previous site on Inns Quay to make way for what would become the new Four Courts building, the Society of King's Inns acquired this site close to Constitution Hill. James Gandon, the architect of the Four Courts building (see **9**, **16**), was also architect for the new King's Inns. The building was begun by Gandon in 1800, but owing to lack of funds the original design was curtailed and the project completed by Francis Johnston in 1817. An unusual aspect of Gandon's design is the north-facing front with Henrietta Street to the rear. In 1825 the Law Library was added to the ensemble of legal buildings. Designed by Frederick Darley, it was located on the site of the former house of the archbishop of Armagh. In 1853 the Ordnance Survey issued a directive from the Phoenix Park to ban the making of tracings of the 1847 plans from the full collection in the library of the King's Inns, a fitting testament to the popularity of the map.

Fig. 8: Linen hall, 1783, by William Hinks (private collection).

7. LINEN HALL AND QUEEN'S INNS

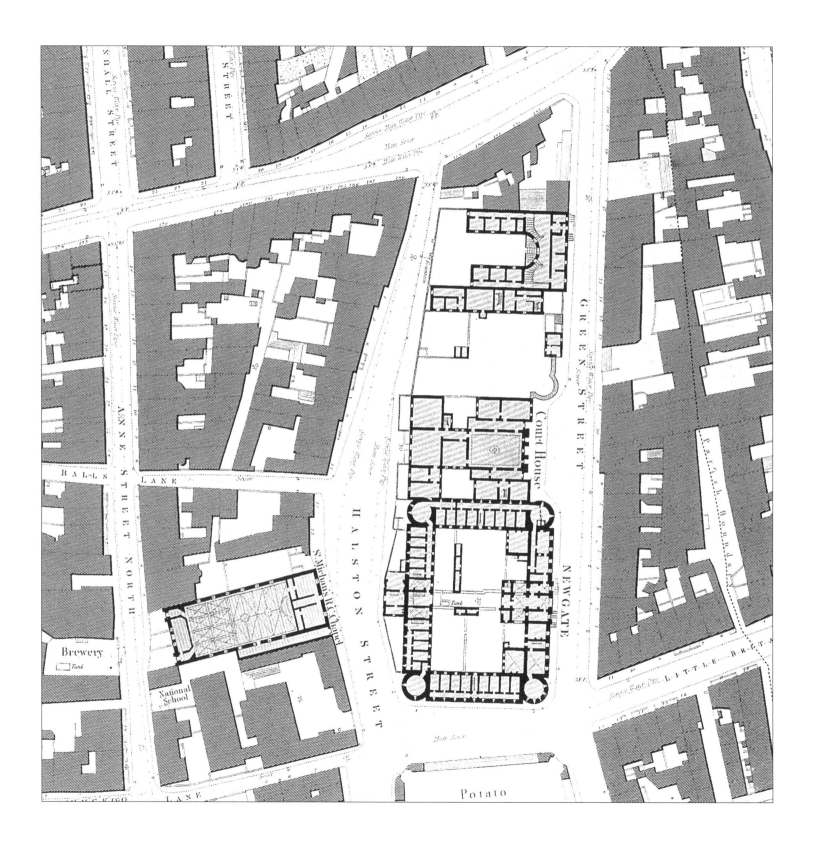

Lodged between Green Street and Halston Street directly south of the Capel Street and King Street North junction was a unique block of penal institutions comprising two prisons, a marshalsea and a courthouse. The site, previously known as Little Green, was completely undeveloped in 1756 when John Rocque surveyed the city. At the extreme south of this block was the infamous Newgate Prison, a solid rectangular building with four imposing towers, one located at each corner (Fig. 9, below). The name of the prison derives from its previous location at one of the city gates near Thomas Street. The sombre granite structure, opened in 1781, stood three storeys in height and conditions within were so dismal that prisoners were forced to beg for alms through the windows from passers-by on the street. The inner courtyard was divided in two by a narrow walled passage leading from the front of the building to the gaoler's house at the rear on Halston Street. The passage provided a point of contact between prisoners and visitors who communicated through iron gates. The building was demolished in 1893 and a public park now occupies the site.

At the northern extremity of the same block was the equally notorious Sheriff's Prison erected in 1794 for those owing debts exceeding ten shillings. In the early years following its establishment, disused chambers in the prison were rented out for business purposes and at one point a vintner's shop was located in the basement. The three-sided courtyard in the centre of the prison was used more often as an improvised ball court, ball alleys being a popular means of recreation at this time. Fortunately this building has managed to survive intact and remains a remarkable example of Dublin's eigh-

teenth-century penal architecture. Immediately south of the prison stood the City Marshalsea (see **40**) for the confinement of individuals owing less than ten shillings. Completing the block and providing a buffer zone between the prison buildings was Green Street Court House, erected in the 1790s and still functioning as a court house today. The architecture is classical in style and the exterior remains unchanged from its original design by Whitmore Davis in 1797. Unusually, Davis chose to give the building two fronts, one on Green Street and one on Halston Street. The Green Street front consists of six large columns of Portland stone supporting a granite pediment. The building is two storeys in height. On the upper storey three large arched windows separate the four inner columns on the portico. The Halston Street front is also classical in style, comprising a less grand portico. Four district courts were held in Green Street throughout the year, including the Quarter Sessions for petty crimes and a court entitled the Court of Oyer and Terminer for more sinister crimes.

Directly opposite the Halston Street entrance to the courthouse stands St Michan's R.C. Chapel. This chapel, built between 1811 and 1814 and still in use today, originally fronted Anne Street North as seen on the map. During the less restrictive period of the late nineteenth century the architect, George Ashlin, was hired to create a more prominent front entrance on Halston Street, with the result that the original entrance on Anne Street North is rarely used today. This reworking of the design provides a good example of changing attitudes towards Catholic church building either side of 1829 when Catholic emancipation was granted.

Fig. 9: Newgate Prison, 1779, from Robert Pool and John Cash, *Views of the most remarkable public buildings … city of Dublin* (Dublin, 1780).

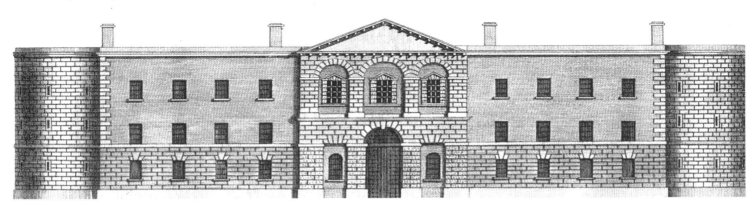

8. KING STREET NORTH

The regulation of markets and fairs during the early decades of the nineteenth century had important repercussions for the topography of Ireland's towns, with new purpose-built market buildings appearing on the map. This is clearly evident in Dublin, particularly in the north inner-city district between Church Street and Capel Street, and north of the quays. West of Church Street the Smithfield cattle and hay market had already set the tone for this neighbourhood, as had Ormond Market east of the Four Courts, in place since 1682 and said to have been one of the first purpose-built markets in Europe. With the passing of the new legislation, the district between these two old markets evolved as market buildings were erected to carry on the bustling trade in provisions that was vital to the city's economy. The two canals, the Royal and the Grand, servicing the north and south sides of the city respectively, ensured a plentiful supply of provisions from all parts of the country, which in turn permitted lower prices. Consequently the markets in Dublin were said to be cheaper than those in London.

Fig. 10: Four Courts and River Liffey, *c.* 1817, by T.S. Roberts (NGI).

The market was very much at the core of Dublin life, as is evident on the 1847 town plan. While primarily dealing in quality meats, Ormond Market also sold poultry, fresh and cured fish, bacon, butter, cheese, fruit and vegetables. The gate to Ormond Market located on Pill Lane was the scene of lively entertainment, as all fish arriving into the city was auctioned from this point. The fish business in the city was carried on mostly by women and the female auctioneer, holding a flat fish by the tail in place of a hammer, sold to the fish women who carried it about the streets in a basket on their heads. This practice led eventually to the establishment of the nearby Fish Market at Boot Lane. Other markets in the vicinity included the fruit market at Anglesea Row, the potato, egg and poultry market at Petticoat Lane, and two vegetable markets at Mary's Lane and May Lane. In addition to the market names, trading activity is borne out in the names of local streets such as Beef Row and Fisher's Lane.

Just west of Ormond Market on King's Inns Quay is one of Dublin's most famous eighteenth-century public buildings, the Four Courts (Fig. 10, above). The Society of King's Inns had occupied this site for centuries before moving to Henrietta Street to allow for the erection of a Thomas Cooley-designed Public Record Office. Cooley began his designs in 1776 and, upon his death in 1784, the project was given a new architect, James Gandon, and a new purpose as the Four Courts (see **7**). The site was not ideal. Being located on a bend of the river its views were restricted, unlike those of the Custom House downstream (see **16**). In order to overcome such shortfalls, Gandon designed an imposing portico of six columns supporting a pediment rising impressively above the Liffey. To compensate for the restricted down and upstream views, a large colonnaded drum and copper dome rose from the building to make what would become an iconic addition to the city skyline.

9. NORTH CITY MARKETS DISTRICT

With the exception of Denmark Street, removed in the late 1970s to make way for the city's first shopping mall, the ILAC Centre, the original ground plan of Sir Humphrey Jervis's seventeenth-century estate from Boot Lane as far as Liffey Street remains intact. In 1757 the work of the Wide Streets Commissioners brought the estate directly in touch with Dublin Castle (see **31**), thus removing its once suburban detachment. By 1847 further street widening and improvement schemes such as the southward extension of Sackville Street to the new Carlisle Bridge (see **13**, **29**) continued to integrate the estate within its urban surroundings. Although the 1847 street plan has little changed from its late seventeenth-century precursor, the topography of the district had evolved considerably with religious, charitable and municipal institutions appearing on the map by the mid-nineteenth century.

The main parish church of St Mary's, situated at the intersection of Stafford Street and Jervis Street, takes its name from the medieval Cistercian abbey, once located upon these lands. This church was built between 1700 and 1704. Early nineteenth-century histories of the city by Warburton, Whitelaw and Walsh, and others were scathing in their criticism of its 'indifferent' architecture and 'mean and dirty' appearance. By 1820 it had fallen into a state of neglect, the original fountains mutilated and discoloured with dirt, and a tower of 'wretched' architecture not deserving of a steeple. The appearance of the building today is plain and minimal (Fig. 11, right). The attached burial ground, now a public park, was ill-suited to the needs of such a large and crowded parish and bodies were often exhumed to make room for new burials. Many influential citizens were buried here, including Mrs Mercer and Mr Simpson, founders of two hospitals that bear their names.

The Scots' Church at the east end of Upper Ormond Quay was built the same year that the town plan was published and was therefore

Fig. 11: St Mary's Church of Ireland, *c.* 1900 (NLI).

added as an update of the original 1838 survey. Farther north along Capel Street was a second Scots' Church, the original entrance to which had been through Meetinghouse Lane just off Mary's Abbey, next to the Jewish synagogue. To improve access a tenement in Capel Street was purchased and renovated to form a long narrow approach into what had once been the rear wall of the church. The neighbouring building was used as a female school. Together with the nearby Presbyterian meeting house on Great Strand Street (the oldest Presbyterian congregation in the city in 1847), this compact cluster of religious institutions between Boot Lane and Jervis Street suggests a strong dissenting tradition in the area. The former Denmark Street site was the location of a Dominican chapel (see **15**) and school house, and a widows' almshouse.

The regulation of Dublin's pharmaceutical industry in the late eighteenth century resulted in the erection in 1791 of the Apothecaries' Hall in Mary Street. The new building was fully fitted out with warehouses and laboratories for the preparation of medicines, which it supplied under licence to apothecaries throughout the city and beyond. Attached to the Apothecaries' Hall was the School of Pharmacy for the examination of candidates aspiring to the rank of master apothecary. Located conveniently to the Apothecaries' Hall just around the corner on Jervis Street was the Charitable Infirmary established originally in 1728 and based in Jervis Street since 1803. The Jervis Street building was mainly a hospital accommodating sixty patients, but also provided room for lectures on medicine, surgery and pharmacy. The infirmary had its own resident apothecary. Opposite the Apothecaries' Hall in Mary Street was the Paving House, headquarters of the Corporation for Paving, Cleansing and Lighting the Streets of Dublin.

10. OLD JERVIS ESTATE

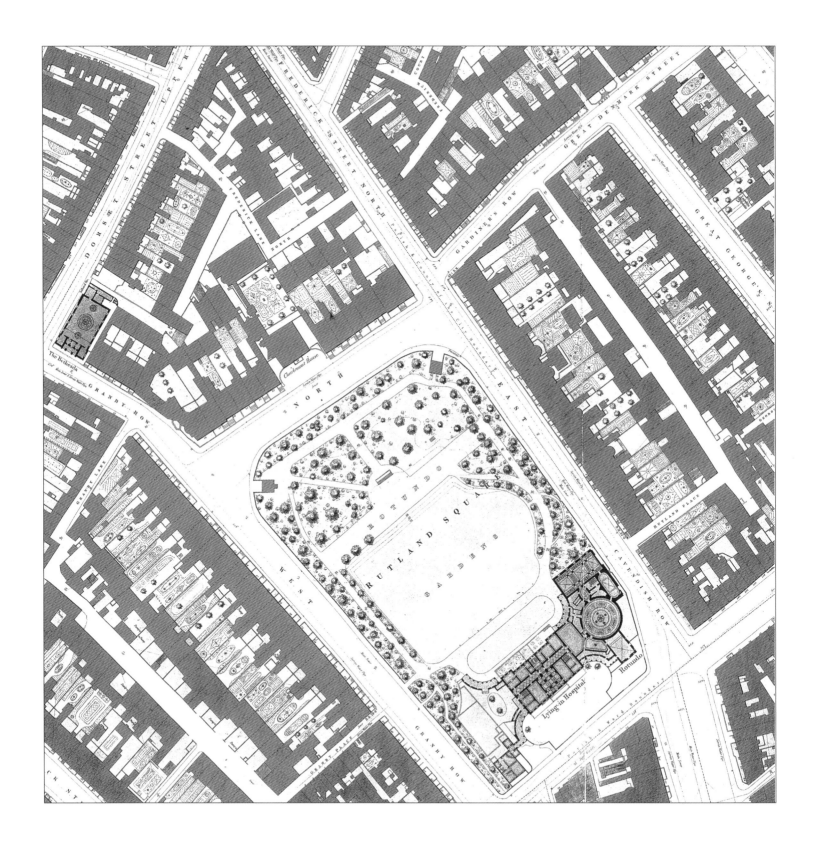

Located at the north end of Sackville Street Upper on the 1847 map, Rutland Square was the creation of Dr Bartholomew Mosse. On this site in 1748 Mosse laid out his new pleasure gardens. Following the model set in London at Vauxhall and Ranelagh with walks and shrubberies, a bowling green and a grand terrace for orchestral performances, the gardens proved very popular with the wealthier citizens, upon whose patronage they thrived. Money raised went towards funding Mosse's new lying-in hospital, which was the principal objective of the scheme. The gardens were opened to the public in 1749 and, soon after, work began on the erection of the hospital at the south end of the site. Designed by Richard Castle, Mosse's hospital was completed in 1757 as the first maternity hospital in the British Isles. With the new addition of a round Assembly Room in 1764, the hospital assumed its present

Fig. 12: Lying-in hospital, 1795, from James Malton, *A picturesque and descriptive view of the city of Dublin* (London, 1792–9).

name, the Rotunda. The newly-added rotunda was used for further charitable entertainments including concerts, card parties, masquerades and balls, collectively described by Malton in the late eighteenth century as the 'most elegant amusements of Dublin' (Fig. 12, above).

The square was surrounded by three terraces on the east, west and north sides, the south side partially facing Sackville Street Upper. It appears likely that a disagreement over property between Mosse and Gardiner prevented the former from locating his gardens and hospital directly presenting onto Sackville Street as originally intended. Gardiner had been keen to develop Cavendish Row as an extension of Sackville Street and had already begun doing so by 1756, as is evident on Rocque's map which shows the north and west sides as yet untouched. No. 9 was purchased by Mosse himself. In 1758 Gardiner's sons began laying out plots on the west side of the square, but these houses were not so large and elaborate as those on the east side. The north side, although designed by John Ensor in 1755, was not developed until the 1760s. When the earl of Charlemont built Charlemont House in 1763 as its centrepiece, the north terrace quickly became one of the most fashionable addresses in the city, known colloquially as Palace Row. Charlemont House today houses the Hugh Lane Municipal Art Gallery.

As the pursuit of leisure lessened in the aftermath of the Act of Union, with many of the city's wealthy residents removing to London, attractions such as pleasure gardens began to lose their appeal. The nearby Marlborough Bowling Green was already gone by 1847. Against the odds, however, Rutland Square managed to retain its charm well into the nineteenth century. Curry, as late as 1835, speaks of gravel walks and shrubberies (as depicted on the 1847 map), in addition to lamp-lit summer evening promenades with military bands in attendance. The calibre of the residents attests to the respectability of the neighbourhood, with none other than former lord mayor, Sir John Kingston James, according to Curry, living in no. 9, the former private residence of Dr Mosse. By 1847 the square was fully developed. On the south-east and south-west sides the names of Cavendish Row and Granby Row refer to the first terrace on either side as far as Rutland and Granby Place. Charlemont House on the north terrace, set in from the other houses, is easily the most distinguishable house on the square. While the earls of Charlemont still resided here in 1847, other residents of Palace Row included the great civil engineer, Sir John MacNeill. The square managed to survive intact until the 1940s.

11. RUTLAND SQUARE

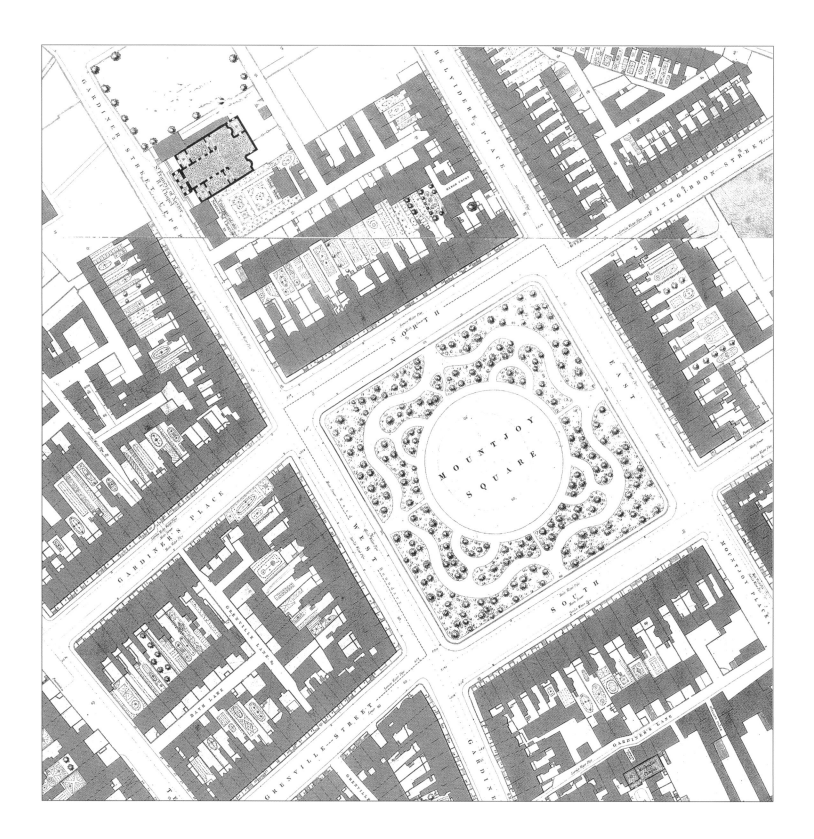

Following the development of Merrion Square in the 1770s on the Fitzwilliam estate on the south side of the city (see **24**), the Gardiner family initiated a similar project on their own estate north of the River Liffey. Mountjoy Square was laid out in the 1780s on the northern fringes of the Gardiner Estate. The street plan surrounding the square put its wealthy residents within convenient reach of the centres of trade and commerce. Via Gardiner Street, Sackville Street and Great Britain Street, key institutions such as the Custom House, Trinity College, Dublin Castle, the linen hall and the King's Inns were easily reached. The choice of location on elevated ground, with splendid views of the Wicklow mountains to the south, added prestige to the new site. The square comprised four terraces of three-storey red-bricked houses presenting onto a railed central garden. The completed square, however, did not match the ambition of the orig-inal design drawn up by Thomas Sherrard, surveyor to the Wide Streets Commissioners in 1787 (Fig. 13, below left). This plan contemplated a much grander scheme, including four palatial façades fronting the terraced houses on each of the square's four sides. Each façade was to include a central entablature with pediment supported by columns below a shallow domed roof. This design proved too expensive and a less elaborate alternative was chosen in its place.

Mountjoy Square was the last of Dublin's Georgian squares to be completed. Like the others it was developed in stages, the north, south and west sides between 1789 and 1798, and the east side not completed until 1809. About fourteen principal developers can be identified with the square's gradual development. These range from builders to landowners, with a cabinet maker and four stuccodors. The involvement of the latter helps to explain the outstanding quality of the plaster work on Mountjoy Square, superior even to that of the houses on Merrion Square. The inner garden, measuring 450 feet from side to side, was enclosed by an iron railing mounted on a dwarf wall of mountain granite. The square was abundantly illuminated with eighty-two fixed iron lamps situated twenty-one feet apart along the railing, in addition to those outside the houses on all four sides. Sherrard's original plan had included the building of a new church for the parish of St George in the centre of the square; this also was discarded for the more affordable option of flowering shrubs and gravel walkways. The new church was eventually built by Francis Johnston in nearby Hardwicke Place between 1802 and 1813. The Catholic Church of St Francis Xavier, Gardiner Street, and the Wesleyan Methodist chapel on Langrish Place, south of Gardiner's Lane, also served the local population.

In 1847 many of the houses on Mountjoy Square and surrounding streets such as Belvidere Place, Grenville Street and Fitzgibbon Street were occupied by barristers and solicitors. This was the post-Union period when the upper echelons of the legal and medical professions had become the new aristocracy. While the medical elite chose Merrion Square, many of the city's legal professionals opted for its north-city counterpart. The location of the King's Inns and new Law Library in Henrietta Street in addition to the Four Courts, all on the north side of the city, may go some way towards explaining this dynamic. The square deteriorated drastically during the latter half of the twentieth century, but recent efforts have been made to save it from ruin.

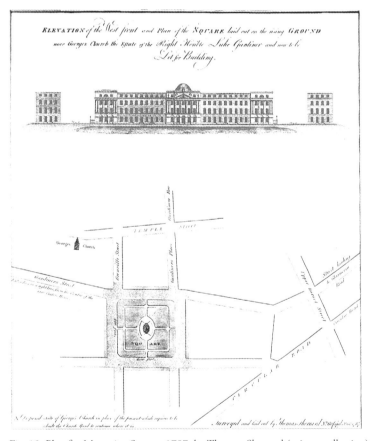

Fig. 13: Plan for Mountjoy Square, 1787, by Thomas Sherrard (private collection).

12. MOUNTJOY SQUARE

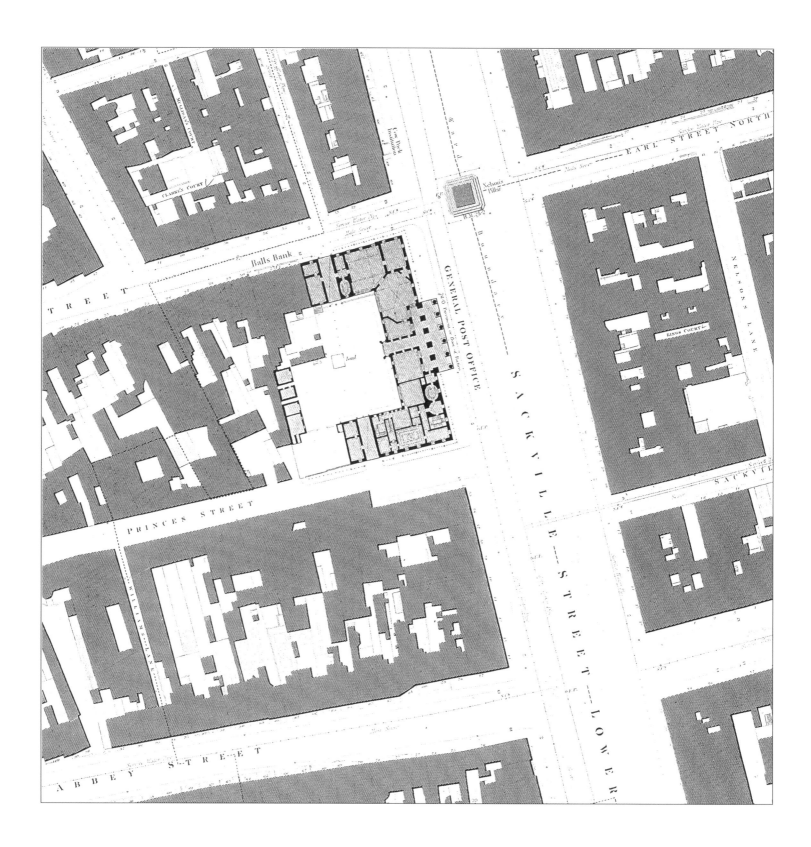

The southward extension of Sackville Mall as far as the River Liffey was one of the most significant projects undertaken by the Wide Streets Commissioners. Laid out during the 1780s and 1790s, the result was an impressively wide and spacious Parisian-style boulevard running from Rutland Square (see **11**) to the newly-built Carlisle Bridge (see **29**). The new thoroughfare, known as Sackville Street after Lionel Cranfield Sackville, 1st duke of Dorset, thus opened the way for traffic between the Gardiner and Fitzwilliam estates north and south of the Liffey. At 150 feet wide it quickly became the centrepiece of the modern city created by the Wide Streets Commissioners.

The extract shows the mid-section of Sackville Street where the lower and upper ends join. On Sackville Street Upper, the Mall, an enclosed rectangular space for public promenade and a feature that gave the street its former name, had been removed by 1847. The first monument to adorn the street was a Grecian Doric column erected in 1808 in honour of Lord Nelson. Known as Nelson's Pillar and depicted on the 1847 plan at the crossroads between Sackville, Henry and Earl Streets, the monument stood 134 feet high, including a thirteen-foot statue of Nelson at the summit (Fig. 14, right). Inside a flight of 168 steps led to an elevated platform 108 feet above the street. From here visitors could avail themselves of an unequalled 360 degree panoramic view of the city. Referred to as the 'Pillar' by generations of Dubliners, the monument provided a focal point for the city's broadest and grandest thoroughfare. In 1966 it was destroyed in an explosion initiated by the Irish Republican Army and had to be removed.

Immediately south-west of Nelson's Pillar stands the iconic General Post Office building designed by Francis Johnston and built between 1814 and 1818 at a cost of £50,000. This splendid building at 223 feet wide comprised the entire block from Henry Street to Princes Street. To the front presenting onto Sackville Street, six large Ionic pillars shown on the map comprise a grand portico eighty feet in height. Three statues of Hibernia, Mercury and Fidelity surmount the pediment. Elaborate stuccoed ceiling work shown on the plan suggests a fine interior. The central aspect is an open courtyard surrounded on three sides, north, south and east, by the building itself, and to the west by the rear gardens of nos 28, 29 and 30 Henry Street. In the centre stood a water tank connected to the main sewer on Henry Street. Arched gateways are shown on either side of the build-

Fig. 14: Sackville Street, 1818, by T.S. Roberts (private collection).

ing, the one to the south on Princes Street for the entrance of mail coaches, that to the north on Henry Street for their departure. Indeed the departure of the mail coaches each evening at seven o'clock excited much attention and crowds gathered in the summer time when the clock struck seven to watch the regimental display. Next to the Henry Street entrance at no. 31 was the bank of Benjamin Ball, a resident of Merrion Square East (see **24**).

By 1847 the gradual transformation of Sackville Street from residential to commercial was all but complete, with only one or two residential properties remaining. The printed 1847 plan names three premises – the Hibernian Bible Society, the Dorset Institution (established in 1815 to provide education and employment for poor females) and the Cow Pock Institution (established in 1804 for administering small-pox vaccines to the poor) – all located on Sackville Street Upper, while the 1843 manuscript plan names five hotels including the Gresham and the Bilton. Invisible on the map, however, is a mixed bunch of high-end commercial establishments and services including jewellers, apothecaries, perfumers, book sellers, hairdressers and peruke makers, cigar and snuff importers, French teachers, wine merchants, circulating libraries, solicitors, tailors, hosier and shirtmakers, a rocking horse manufacturer, a music teacher and a furrier, among others.

13. SACKVILLE STREET LOWER

Abbey Street Lower, stretching from Sackville Street Lower to Beresford Place, was an interesting street containing a number of religious, commercial and cultural institutions. Starting at the west section of the street was Union Chapel, whose name was derived from the union of two smaller Presbyterian congregations thought to have connections with Skinners Alley and Tailors Hall. Around 1818 the two congregations amalgamated before eventually moving to the new Presbyterian Union Chapel in Abbey Street Lower in 1825. Five years earlier the neighbouring Wesleyan Methodist chapel had also established itself on the same street two doors to the east. Crossing over the Marlborough Street junction the Music Hall occupied the site between nos 12 and 13. This large and impressive building, previously known as the Circus, had been used to stage equestrian and dramatic performances. A magnificent chandelier suspended from the centre of the ceiling dominated the entire room, lighting up the galleries on all sides. An illustration shows the interior in 1844 (Fig. 15, below right). The four skylights shown are also visible in the detail of the map. Next to the Music Hall was the Dublin Savings Bank and George Papworth's Baptist chapel of 1839 (see **17**, **29**, **32** for more of Papworth's work). The chapel had a relatively short history since it was sold in 1891 and thereafter fitted out as a shop. Opposite the chapel on the south side of Abbey Street Lower was the Northumberland Market and east of that, just off the extract, were the Northumberland Baths.

Moving back down the street in a westerly direction towards Sackville Street, the next premises of importance was the Mechanics Institute, originally established in 1824 to promote the scientific education of artisans and journeymen. Having previously occupied premises in Sackville Street and the Royal Exchange, the institute towards the end of the 1840s purchased the old Princess Theatre at 27 Abbey Street Lower. The former theatre was capable of holding 2,000 people and was considered well-suited to the needs of the expanding institute. Elaborate in style, a square lamp-lit porch can be seen on the map fronting onto Abbey Street. The idea was to provide scientific and technical instruction in the form of lectures and demonstrations for the working classes as an alternative to the traditional classically dominated syllabus. The institute, with over 2,700 members, had its own library of more than 3,000 volumes.

Crossing back over Marlborough Street, the final building of cultural distinction on Abbey Street Lower was that of the Royal Hibernian Academy of Painting, Sculpture and Architecture. The academy, founded in Dublin in 1823, owes its origins to the architect, Francis Johnston, its founder and first president (see **4**, **7**, **13**, **19**, **30**, **31**, **42**, **43** for more examples of Johnston's prolific work). In addition to purchasing the site for the academy in Abbey Street Lower, Johnston designed the new three-storey building with the symbolic heads of Palladio, Michael Angelo and Raphael adorning the front and representing the academy's three main areas of interest – architecture, sculpture and painting. The interior is depicted in detail on the map and with the help of contemporary descriptions it is possible to recreate the layout of the building. Inside the main entrance was a grand vestibule and an impressive flight of steps leading to a wide exhibition room for works in water colour. An arched entrance to the rear of this room led to a larger and longer saloon for works in oil. Off to the right of this great room was the sculpture gallery, a newly-added octagonal room. Owing to its proximity to the General Post Office, the building was destroyed in 1916 during the Easter Rising.

Fig. 15: Music Hall, from *Illustrated London News*, 20 Jan. 1844 (NLI).

14. ABBEY STREET LOWER

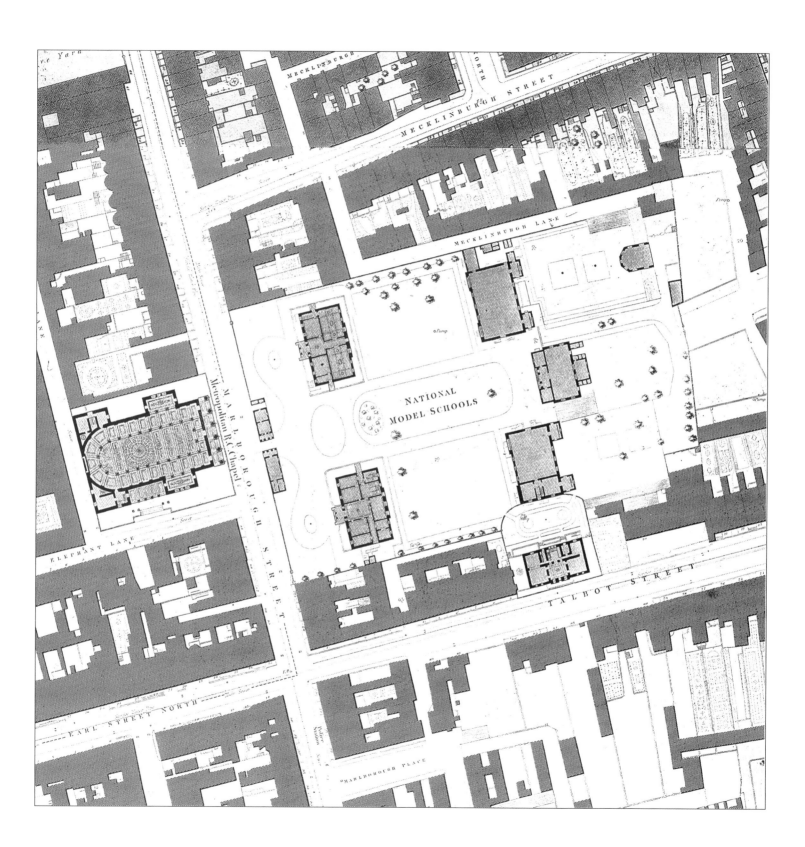

Fig. 16: Tyrone House, 1779, from Robert Pool and John Cash, *Views of the most remarkable public buildings ... city of Dublin* (Dublin, 1780).

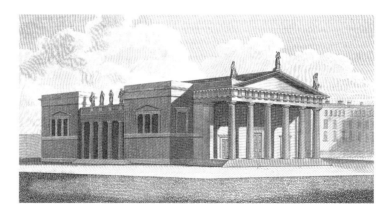

Fig. 17: St Mary's Pro-Cathedral, 1817, from Warburton *et al.*, *History of the city of Dublin* (London, 1818).

The National Model Schools shown in this extract were located on the site of the present Department of Education in Marlborough Street. The site was originally developed by Marcus Beresford, Viscount Tyrone, where in 1740 he built Tyrone House as his town residence. This house was designed by Richard Castle and consisted of two storeys with attic over a basement. 'Robust and sober' best describes Castle's design, the only flourish being the Venetian window above the front porch (Fig. 16, above left). The most notable feature of the interior is Castle's grand mahogany staircase and the beautiful stucco work attributed to the Lafranchini brothers. By 1835 the house had fallen into disrepair and was sold along with the adjoining five acres to the Commissioners for National Education for the sum of £7,000.

The commissioners had been established in 1831 following the suggestion of the chief secretary, Edward Stanley, for a system of state-funded teacher training and model or practice schools based on that pioneered by the Kildare Place Society in the 1820s. Boarding facilities were provided for student teachers and the new system advocated the coming together of Catholics and Protestants in the one classroom. The commissioners established the first model schools on the Marlborough Street site and rolled out the system nationwide thereafter. Suspicion from the Catholic hierarchy resulted in the banning of Catholic attendance in 1863. The 1847 map shows a site transformed from residential to institutional, with the original Tyrone House located in the south-west corner augmented by new buildings.

A replica of Tyrone House was built directly north of the original with a central mall running from west to east between the two matching buildings. Located at the east end of this mall was the new infant model school flanked on either side by the girls' school to the north and boys' school to the south. The building on the south side of the complex on Talbot Street was used for the training of female teachers.

On the opposite side of Marlborough Street, facing the central mall of the National Model Schools, was St Mary's Metropolitan R.C. Chapel, also known as St Mary's Pro-Cathedral, still standing today (Fig. 17, above right). When viewing the whole, it can be seen that the replica Tyrone House was designed to provide symmetry with its original counterpart and the facing chapel. The Pro-Cathedral was built between 1814 and 1825 and, although the architect remains unknown, the style is French after the basilican church of St Philippe du Roule in Paris. The principal motivator for this project was Archbishop Troy of Dublin, a Dominican friar and previously associated with St Mary's Dominican chapel in Denmark Street (see **10**). Troy established a building committee to raise funds for the replacement of the old St Mary's with a larger more central church. The committee eventually acquired the site of Annesley House, Marlborough Street, former town house of the Annesleys of Castlewellan, Co. Down. Over the past two centuries the Pro-Cathedral has played a central role in the formation of the Irish state, hosting the funerals of such eminent figures as Daniel O'Connell, Michael Collins and Eamon de Valera.

15. MARLBOROUGH STREET

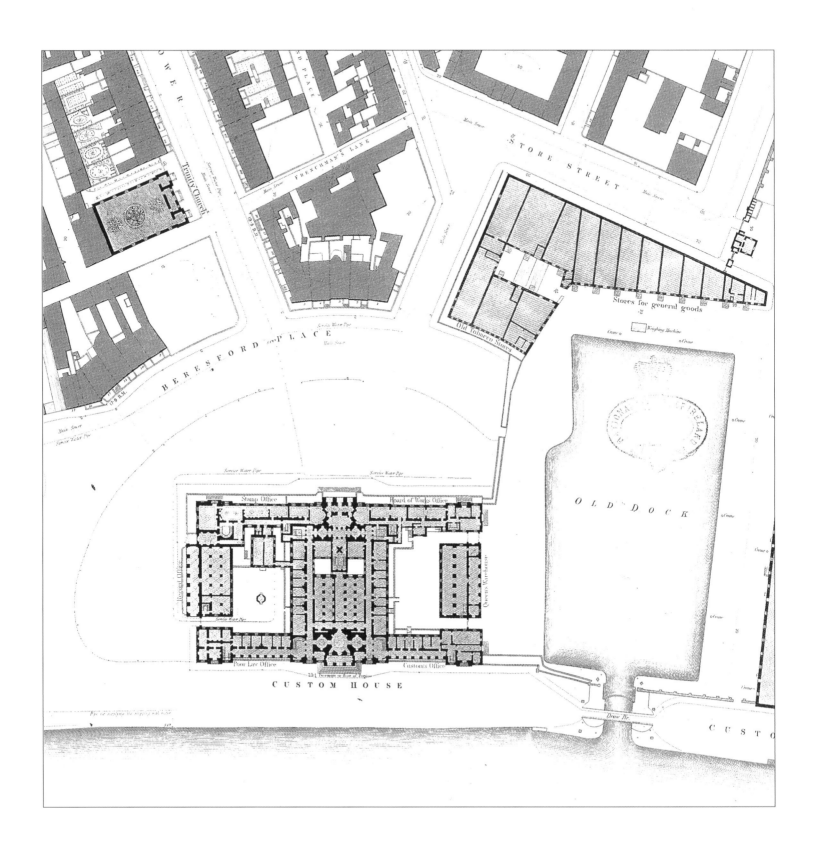

In 1770 John Beresford, a Dublin politician and MP for Co. Waterford, was appointed commissioner of the revenue by the lord lieutenant, Lord Townsend. This appointment was pivotal to the future planning and development of the port area and the wider city of Dublin. As revenue commissioner he was responsible for having the site of the Custom House moved downstream from its cramped location on Essex Quay (see **28**).

The site for the new Custom House was a spacious plot of waste ground at the western end of the North Wall. James Gandon was the chosen architect and the new building was completed to his design in 1785 at a cost of £250,000 (Fig. 18, right). Gandon's masterpiece has been recognised as probably the greatest of Dublin's eighteenth-century neo-classical buildings. The edifice was designed with four front views and forms a large quadrangle measuring 375 feet by 205 feet. The style is of the Doric order with columns and friezes. The south front facing the river is the grandest with a magnificent portico below a copper dome, upon which stands a twelve-foot statue of Hope resting on her anchor. Standing above the four pillars of the portico are four statues, Neptune, Plenty, Industry and Mercury, and the symbolism continues with a relief carved in the pediment of the friendly union of Britannia and Hibernia. The keystones represent the rivers of Ireland with Anna Livia, the only female head, representing the city.

Within the building were the offices of numerous government departments, not all related to revenue. Conveniently located to the south front facing the river were the Emigration Office, Landing Surveyor's Office, Landing Watch Office, Searcher's Office, Sample Office, Register Office and storerooms. On the opposite north front were the Stamp Office, Commissary General's Office and the Board of Public Works Office. The west end of the building contained a record office, while the opposite east end comprised a large warehouse and an engine house. Located within the central block between the two courtyards were the excise office, permit office and His Majesty's Stationery Office, in addition to more storerooms including stores for 'old books and documents' as labelled on the Ordnance Survey 1836 preliminary plans.

Today Beresford's legacy remains in the street name directly to the rear of the Custom House. When laid out by the Wide Streets Commissioners in 1792 Beresford Place formed a crescent around the north, east and part of the west side of the Custom House, with two openings onto Gardiner Street and Store Street. The central block of houses still surviving was built for Beresford under Gandon's design. Those west of Gardiner Street, though grand in design, unfortunately

Fig. 18: Custom House and River Liffey, 1817, by T.S. Roberts (NGI).

fell victim to the colossally invasive Loop Line Railway Bridge in 1889. However, the excellent planning opportunity that Beresford Place presented was already lost before the building of this bridge when the east side of the crescent was assigned to warehousing, eventually giving way to a bus station in 1946. Directly east of the Custom House was the Old Dock built in the same year as Beresford Place. This dock communicated with the Liffey via a lock and was capable of receiving the largest vessels in the early nineteenth century. Nonetheless, with the transition from sail to steam and the subsequent increase in vessel size and power, the dock was superfluous to the needs of the port by the end of the nineteenth century and in 1927 it was filled in to make way for further warehousing (see **17**).

16. BERESFORD PLACE

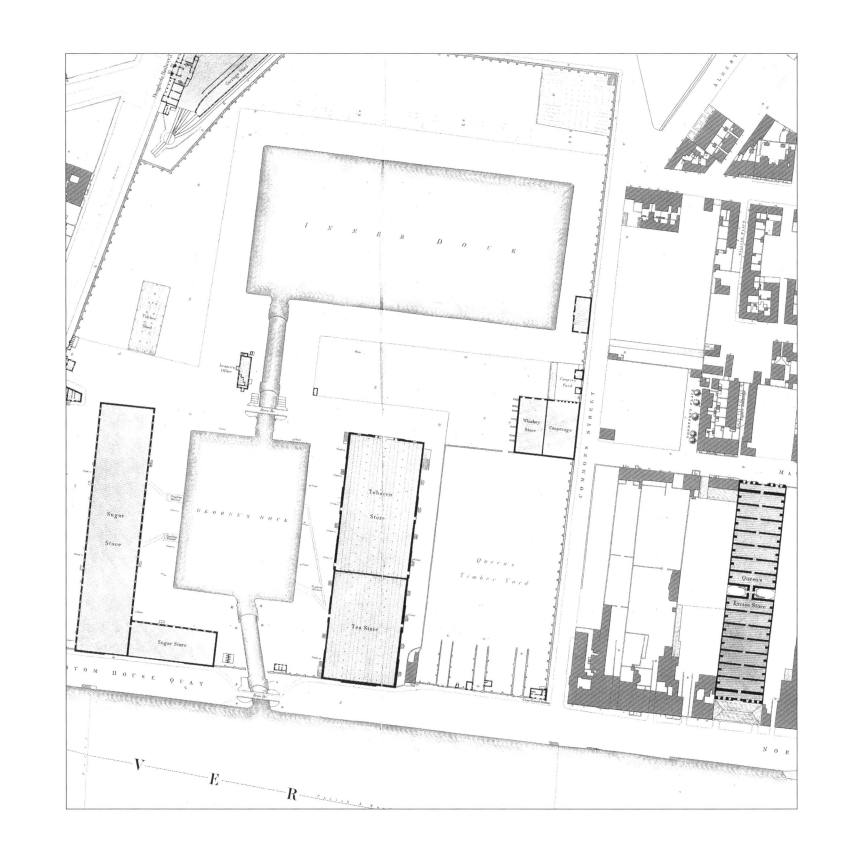

The Custom House Quay and North Wall were the epicentre of the commercial and industrial port in the mid-nineteenth century (Fig. 19, below). Following the erection of the new Custom House building in 1785 (see **16**) and the opening of the adjacent Old Dock in 1796, the modern nineteenth-century port began to take shape. In as little as four years between 1820 and 1824 the Custom House complex was built with new docks and modern bonded warehouses, all enclosed within a high security wall. Many of the works carried out during this prolific period were designed by John Rennie, who had also built the Old Dock in 1796. These included the tobacco store built in 1820, George's Dock opened in 1821 and the Inner Dock opened in 1824. In addition to his work in Dublin Port, Rennie is associated with the building of Howth and Kingstown harbours along with his son, Sir John Rennie, who also enjoyed an esteemed career in engineering.

As only goods liable for customs duty were received in the Custom House docks, the new tea, sugar and tobacco stores were of importance. From the evidence on the Ordnance Survey 1836 sketch plan it would appear that the smaller George's Dock was used for the loading and unloading of vessels and weighing of goods, since eight cranes are shown around the dock. Three weighing scales are also shown, two on the east side next to the sugar stores and one on the west side next to the tobacco stores. The larger Inner Dock, surrounded by metal, stone and wooden posts, was used for mooring with only two cranes marked on the plan. Entry to each dock was through a narrow lock via a swivel bridge. As vessels grew in size over the coming decades the entrance rendered the new docks obsolete by mid-century, yet they were considered a great triumph on their opening in 1821. Rennie's tobacco store, a high, single-storey over vaulted basement building still stands today, although substantially reworked as a modern shopping mall. Also known as Stack A Warehouse, it was used in 1856 as an enormous banquet hall to honour the Irish regiments who had just returned from the Crimean War. Over 3,500 guests and 1,000 paying spectators were present, so large a crowd that no other building in Dublin was deemed suitable for the occasion. The sugar store west of George's Dock was built in 1824, although work was ongoing after this date since it is marked as 'not finished' on the Ordnance Survey 1836 preliminary plan. While part of this building still survives as a bank, it is totally unrecognisable from its original format.

Immediately east of Stack A was the Queen's Timber Yard, in the south-east corner of which was located a coast guard station. Farther east, completing the ensemble of bonded warehouses though outside the walls of the Custom House yard, was the Queen's Excise Store. This building still survives and, although built in 1821 as His Majesty's Excise Store, it is named on the 1847 map in acknowledgement of Queen Victoria.

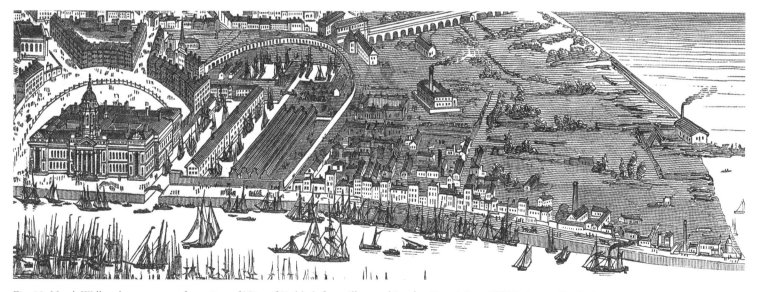

Fig. 19: North Wall and port, extract from view of 'City of Dublin', from *Illustrated London News*, 1 June 1846 (private collection).

17. CUSTOM HOUSE QUAY

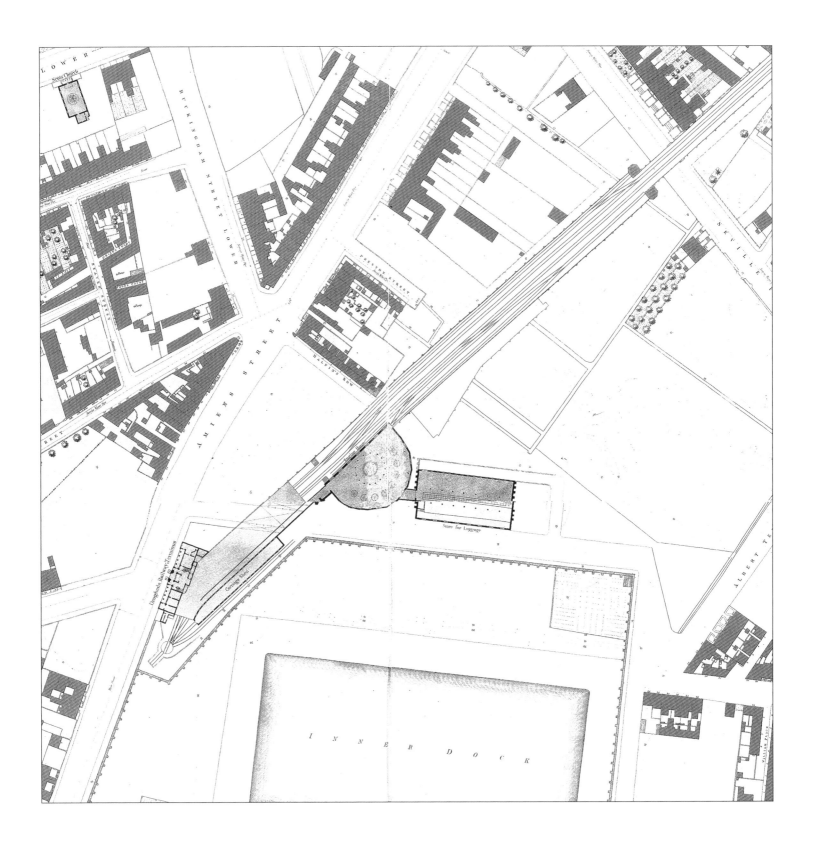

The Dublin and Drogheda Railway was incorporated by an act of parliament on 13 August 1836. Construction began in 1840 and the line was opened for business on 24 May 1844. It was Dublin's second railway after the Dublin and Kingstown line, which had opened in 1834. During this development process the Ulster Railway from Belfast to Armagh was also under construction and it was the intention of both companies that the two lines should eventually meet to form a through route between the northern and southern metropolises. The engineer chosen for the job was William Cubitt, who went on to design the Crystal Palace in Hyde Park for the Great Exhibition of 1851. Cubitt had been employed at various times by the port authorities in Dublin and Belfast for work on both harbours. During his work on the Drogheda line he stayed in the Gresham Hotel as a guest of the owner, Thomas Gresham, who was also one of the railway's original promoters.

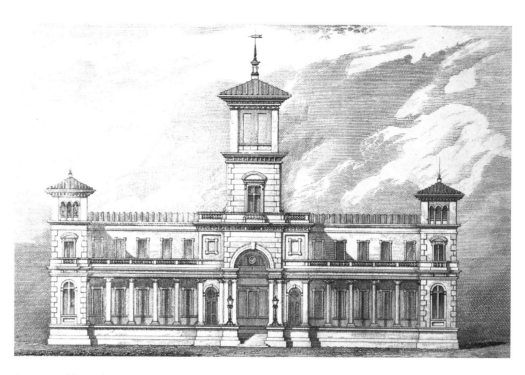

Fig. 20: Dublin and Drogheda Railway terminus, Amiens Street, from *Hand book to the Dublin and Drogheda Railway* (Dublin, 1844).

The 1847 plan shows the Drogheda Railway terminus on a site in the north-west corner of the Custom House yard, immediately south of Sheriff Street. This site was owned by the government, which leased it to the Scovel brothers who in turn sub-leased it to the Custom House (see **16**, **17**). In an effort towards improvement, the government sold its interest in this land to the railway company as it was felt that a new railway terminus would make a pleasing addition to the architecture of this run-down district. For the railway company the advantage was a more convenient location, with easier access to the city than another proposed site north of Sheriff Street. Indeed the original intentions of the promoters had been to site their terminus in Sackville Street opposite the General Post Office, in the heart of the city. This was to be achieved by crossing Amiens Street and cutting through a long swathe of dense housing separating Talbot Street and Abbey Street Lower. The plan was hampered for a number of reasons, not least of which was the cost of compensation.

The terminus was the last part of the works to be completed (Fig. 20, above). On the same date that the railway opened for business the lord lieutenant laid the first stone of the new building. Designed by William Deane Butler and built by Williams and Sons of nearby Talbot Street, the original building is a balanced composition of two storeys below a central campanile and flanked on either end by miniature campanili. The façade is of native Irish granite from the quarries of Golden Hill in County Wicklow. The 1847 map shows the engine house and luggage store located north of Sheriff Street, with the carriage shed south of the street to the rear of the main terminus, which formed, and still does, a noble termination to the vista from Sackville Street via Talbot Street.

18. AMIENS STREET RAILWAY TERMINUS

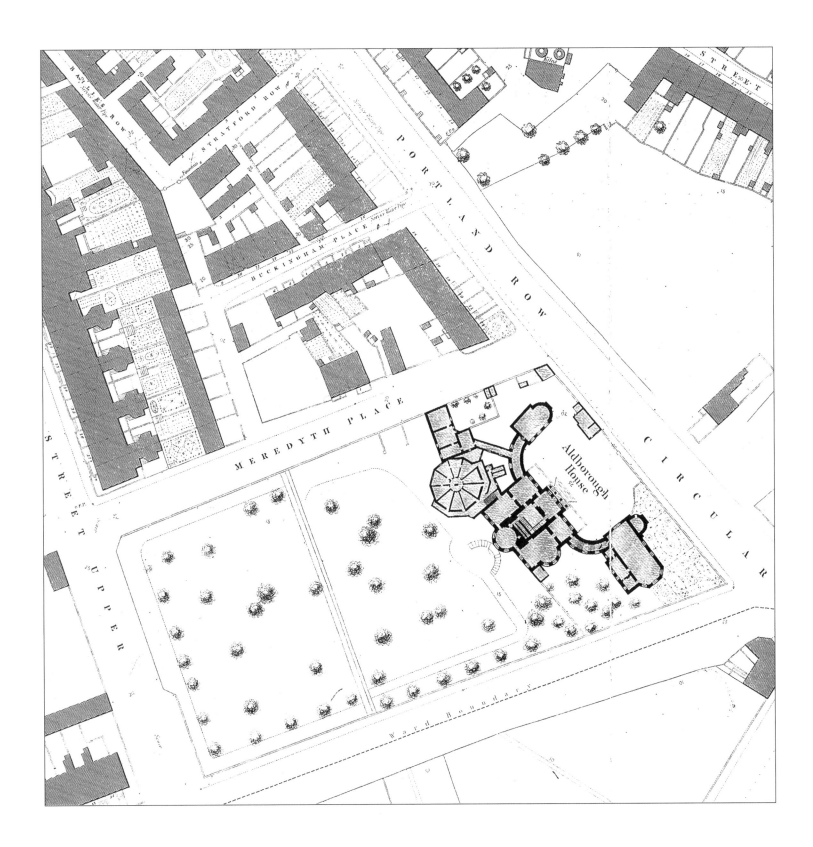

Aldborough House was the last of the great mansions of eighteenth-century Dublin (Fig. 21, below). Built for Edward Augustus Stratford, 2nd earl of Aldborough, it was completed in 1798, but sadly never fulfilled its intended role as the Aldborough family home. Stratford was a great patron of the arts. Eccentric and highly educated, he was also ostentatious by nature with a weakness for spending beyond his means. He was responsible for laying out Stratford Place in London, upon which he built the splendid Stratford House and in the process lost a large amount of money. In Dublin he had inherited some undeveloped lands on the North Circular Road near North Strand and in 1792 he set about building on them another elaborate mansion. The idea was to compete with and outdo Lord Belvedere's mansion at nearby Great Denmark Street.

Although the area chosen was completely undeveloped, Stratford was confident that, once built, his new house would attract further fashionable development in the area and with this in mind he laid out new streets including Stratford Row. This never happened for various reasons. Owing to financial difficulties that appeared to plague Stratford in all his business activities, the house took far longer to complete than it should have. In addition, Stratford himself ended up spending six weeks in Newgate Prison (see **8**) having lost a libel case against Lord Clare. Within four years of the house being finished, both Stratford and his wife had died leaving no children. A lengthy legal wrangle between the heirs apparent resulted in the house being eventually auctioned in 1813 to Professor von Feinaigle to be used as a school. By 1843 it had become a temporary army barracks and after that a post office depot.

In the early years of the construction process the eminent architect Francis Johnston had been involved, but money problems led to him resigning from the project. Nevertheless, the design was most elaborate and comprised among other things a library, a music room, a chapel, a theatre and a refreshment room. It would be tempting to say no expense was spared in designing the house, but insufficient finances continually hampered the building process and close inspection of the plaster work and other interior design features reveals that finer details were sacrificed for the sake of economy. On the map a new extension is shown on the north side of the main block, west of the chapel wing. Farther west against the north wall can be seen an unnamed ball court, most probably added when the house functioned as a temporary army barracks since a number of ball courts were located in or near barracks and prisons in the city during this period. The large landscaped garden to the rear of the house was taken in the 1940s to build public housing. It is unfortunate that Stratford's Dublin mansion has not been treated as kindly over time as its London counterpart. Now derelict and boarded up, the building strikes a forlorn and shameful image of neglect.

Fig. 21: Aldborough House, late eighteenth cent., by William Skelton (private collection).

19. ALDBOROUGH HOUSE

In 1800 George Halpin senior was appointed Inspector of Works for the Corporation for Preserving and Improving the Port of Dublin. In 1830 his son, George junior, was appointed as his assistant and eventually succeeded his father as chief engineer. For a period of over sixty years from 1800 to 1861 both men were responsible for the maintenance and upkeep of the port of Dublin. By the 1830s berthing facilities within the port were inadequate and not only were ships becoming damaged along the quay walls, but also increased traffic demanded that those awaiting quay space were forced to moor in the bay. This dangerous practice led to the loss of many ships, since cross winds could be treacherous and ships often ran aground during low water. To remedy this ill, the decision was taken to dredge a deep-water basin along the East Wall at the eastern extremity of the port. This became known as Halpin's Pond and it was further deepened and extended in the 1840s to a depth of sixteen feet at low water. For the time being, large vessels coming into the port could moor and discharge into lighter vessels using this new facility.

The dredging of Halpin's Pond represents the earliest step in the development of the modern deep-water port. The 1847 map shows a patent slip north-east of the unnamed Halpin's Pond. By mid-century this slip had become inadequate owing to the increasing size of the steam vessels operating in the port. In 1849 the Dublin Chamber of Commerce called for its replacement and the port consulted the London engineer, James Walker, who two years previously had completed the cutting of the Victoria Channel in Belfast harbour. Walker carried out his investigations, which confirmed the port's suitability for a new graving dock. George Halpin junior put forward a plan for a dock to be built close to the old slip, using cofferdams. The plan re-ceived the backing of William Cubitt, another eminent London engineer who frequently acted as consulting engineer for the port. The contract was given to William Dargan, who completed the task in 1860. During the construction process a retaining wall 2,300 feet in length was built to enclose a large amount of water surrounding the pond. The beginnings of this wall are shown on the map and the reclaimed land within this enclosure became the foundations of the modern port.

Seven years after the publication of the 1847 town plan a significant appointment was made in Dublin port when the young Bindon Blood Stoney was hired as assistant engineer to George Halpin junior. Stoney's pioneering work in the port over the next forty years, and the modest budget upon which he carried it out, helped to secure his reputation as one of the most resourceful and skilful engineers in the country. Halpin's Pond had never been thought of as more than a temporary measure and by the late 1860s it was ineffective in dealing with the larger vessels and heavier traffic. It was against this background that Stoney first presented his proposal for the North Wall extension and deep-water basin using large concrete blocks of 350 tons in weight to be floated from the quayside and placed on the basin floor by means of a purpose-built vessel and crane known as a floating shears, which Stoney himself had designed. Original, cost-saving and daring, the proposal proved successful – so much so that the British Association for the Advancement of Science, meeting in Dublin in 1876, visited the port to view the works in progress. Within five years of his initial appointment as assistant engineer, Stoney had taken complete charge of the port.

20. PATENT SLIP AND HALPIN'S POND

The Hibernian Marine School located on Sir John Rogerson's Quay between Lime Street and Cardiff Lane was established by parliamentary grant in 1775 (Fig. 22, right). Its objective was to provide maintenance, education and apprenticeships for the children of seamen. In the early years of its existence the school maintained up to 150 boys annually, but these figures fell off after 1830 when the school's parliamentary grant was withdrawn. In the endowed schools report of 1857 it was shown in an unfavourable light with poor diet, insufficient clothing and the lack of bathroom and water closet facilities being listed among other problems. By 1857 enrolment figures had fallen to twenty-seven, a number that must presumably have been lost in the spacious playground depicted to the rear on the 1847 map.

South-west of the Marine School and close to the gas works, the Mariners' Church on Forbes Street has an interesting history. This church was erected in 1832 to replace its predecessor, the Episcopal Floating Chapel, which had been located nearby in the Grand Canal Basin since 1822. During a period of intense religious zeal, floating chapels became commonplace in the port districts of the larger towns, with Belfast, Liverpool and London similarly administering to the spiritual needs of their seafaring communities. The floating chapel had its own chaplain, whose duty in addition to performing divine service on the vessel in Ringsend was to visit other ships frequenting the port. By the 1830s the vessel used for this purpose had become old and decayed and the decision was taken to replace it with a more permanent structure on solid ground. The Mariners' Church, including school rooms, cost £2,000 to erect and was capable of accommodating up to 500 people. It was opened in 1833 and, in addition to normal Sunday services, lectures were held on Wednesday and Friday evenings.

Directly south of the Marine School north of Great Brunswick Street was Queen's Square (the present Pearse Square). Begun in 1839 by Peter Martin, a builder who resided on the square, this develop-

ment of thirty-nine houses consisted of a railed garden surrounded by three terraces on its north, east and west sides. The south side was open to Great Brunswick Street. The most unusual aspect of Queen's Square in 1847 was the class of its residents, who, living in the shadow of the nearby gas works, represented an oasis of culture in the most unlikely of settings. Artists and musicians were numerous in this small residential enclave. At nos 6, 10 and 15, on the west side of the square, were John Kane and William Murphy, both professors of music, and Frederick Lyster, teacher of piano and vocals. At nos 5 and 11 were the artist, Thomas Bishop and the sculptor, Constantine

Fig. 22: Marine School, Sir John Rogerson's Quay, 1796, from James Malton, *A picturesque and descriptive view of the city of Dublin* (London, 1792–9).

Panormo. While the north side was unoccupied during this period, the east side was even more colourful with respect to its residents. At no. 46 was Augustus Cesar Maranni, professor of Spanish and Italian at Trinity College. Three doors down was another music professor, James Rogers at no. 49, while at no. 51 were members of the Corri family of Edinburgh, a well-known musical family of Italian descent. In this house, Haydn, Henry and Eugene Corri, each an accomplished musician and composer, and Valentine Corri, an artist and sculptor, all resided. At no. 56 on the same side was William Hodges, professor of piano.

21. ST MARK'S MARITIME QUARTER

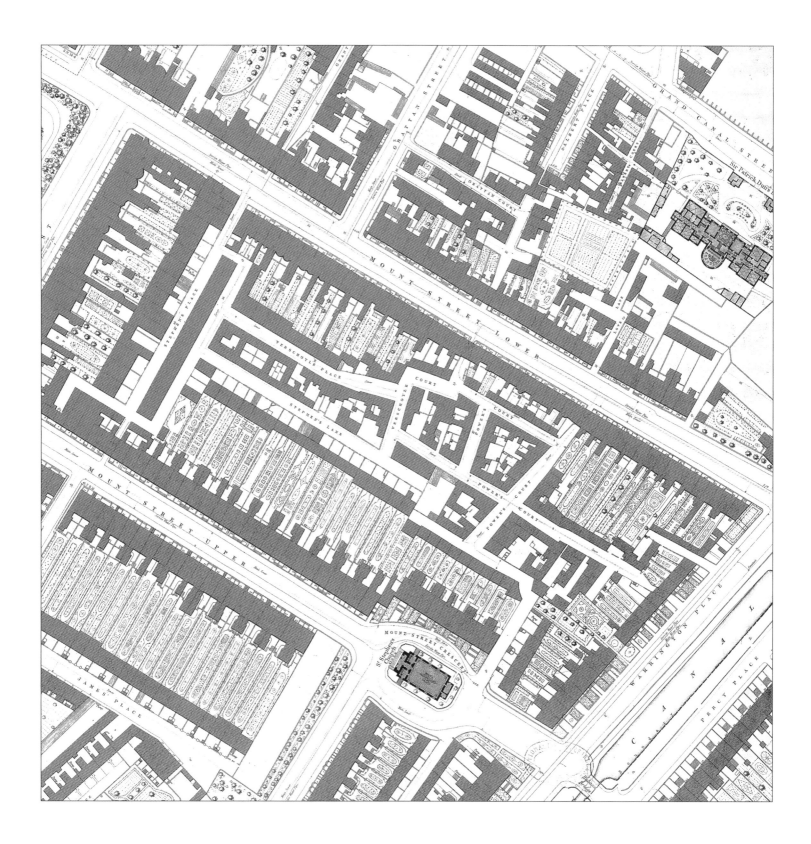

A well-documented topographical feature of nineteenth-century Dublin was the notorious slums that lurked behind the respectable thoroughfares. This feature of the city is captured in extraordinary detail on the 1847 plan. Scores of alleys, lanes, courts and rows depict the underbelly of the elegant city, where dairy yards, huxters' shops and tenements occupied a maze of dilapidated buildings hidden from view. The tightly-packed area of Power's Court, Verschoyle Court and Stephen's Lane, enclosed within a four-sided block of graceful town houses fronting Mount Street Upper and Lower, Warrington Place and the highly sought-after Merrion Square East (see **24**) as depicted on the map extract, provides a fascinating example of luxury and poverty in surprisingly close proximity.

In this densely packed neighbourhood three names are predominant: Verschoyle, Power and Stephen, the first less difficult to trace than the latter two. This name comes from Richard Verschoyle, a wealthy merchant who married Barbara Fagan in 1790; it was as Mrs Verchoyle that Barbara Fagan continued her family tradition of managing the Fitzwilliam estates, acting as the estate agent for Viscount Fitzwilliam during some of the most exciting developments the city was ever to know. Her father, Bryan Fagan, had been responsible for laying out Merrion Square in the mid-eighteenth century; Barbara would be the estate agent who oversaw its embellishment. Her husband's name, Verschoyle, first appears associated with this particular lane in a deed of 1817. Of thirty-one properties listed in the 1847 directory for these two narrow back lanes, with the exception of a spirit dealer, two provisions dealers and three laundresses, all of the rest were in tenements. In the adjacent stretch of adjoining laneways

known as Power's Court, thirty-five of fifty-three were in tenements and nine in stables, along with provisions dealers, vintners and a bell ringer. In close proximity to Verschoyle Place and Court was Stephen's Place, in which was located the well-known Whitsitt and Watson's coach factory, managed in 1847 by Mrs Whitsitt. Situated among the tenements to the rear of the factory on Stephen's Lane was that of Michael M'Evoy's blacksmiths.

In such tightly-packed areas within the city, sanitation was a major concern for the various authorities. Indeed the growing preoccupation with health in towns during this period may well have been an important spur towards completing the large-scale map of Dublin in 1847. The surveyors worked in conjunction with the Commissioners for Paving in order to come up with an appropriate system for exhibiting sewers, water pipes, fireplugs, turn cocks and gratings. In the accompanying extract, enclosed underground sewers can be seen running along some of these lanes with open drains also shown. Yet other lanes such as Stephen's Lane and Verschoyle Court lack any sanitary facilities. Water supply also appears to have been a problem, with one fountain on Verschoyle Court connected to the water mains for Mount Street Lower supplying ninety-eight separate properties. For the barristers and solicitors occupying the surrounding residences on Mount Street Lower and Upper, and particularly for the elite occupants of Merrion Square East, the lack of a proper water supply and sewage system was not a prevailing issue, and the 'marginalised' families occupying the back lanes out of sight of the lavish town houses were somehow at a comfortable distance.

22. VERSCHOYLE AND POWER'S COURTS

The present street frontage of Pearse Station on Westland Row bears no resemblance to its appearance in 1834 when the Dublin and Kingstown Railway opened. The original design by Charles Vignoles was for a terminus rather than a station, the starting point on the proposed railway to Kingstown (Fig. 23, below, shows trains leaving the rear of the station). The style was Italianate with a two-storey façade of seven bays and three pedestrian entrances onto the main street. However, the extension of the railway in 1891 to link up with the Great Northern Railway at Amiens Street, via an elevated line crossing the Liffey in front of the Custom House (see **16**), permanently altered the appearance of the Westland Row station.

The Dublin and Kingstown Railway was the first passenger railway in Ireland and was the brainchild of James Pim junior. Pim was a member of the well-known Quaker family prominent in the Dublin business world of the mid-nineteenth century. The same family went on to open Pim's department store in South Great George's Street and was also responsible for building the splendid George's Street market and arcade. Other business interests included the financing of Charles Wye Williams's City of Dublin Steam Packet Company during this period. James was a merchant and banker and, together with his banking partners, he provided £17,000 of the capital required to establish the railway. Five other members of the Pim family invested substantial sums, but it was the dogged determination of James that finally succeeded in obtaining a crucial loan of £100,000 from the, at first unenthusiastic, Board of Works. The security of this loan was vital to encouraging further investment, thus making it possible for the project to reach completion. The primary and initial purpose of the railway was to link the harbour at Kingstown, then used by the post office packet ships (with which the Pims had financial interests), with the city of Dublin. This would allow for a speedier and more efficient mail service between Dublin and London, an issue of substantial importance to Westminster during the nineteenth century. As early as 1802 the engineer of Kingstown Harbour, John Rennie, had mooted a Dublin and Kingstown ship canal connecting with the Grand Canal harbour for the same purpose, but the idea was rejected by Dublin Port and quickly became impractical with the advent of railway communication.

Next to the railway terminus was St Andrew's Catholic Chapel. This building more than any other Catholic chapel in the city serves as a monument to the passing of the Catholic Emancipation Act in 1829. A less conspicuous parish church, already in the process of being built, was abandoned in 1832 in favour of the more prominent Westland Row site. As seen on the map, the chapel with attached presbyteries and school was grand in scale, and the building of the complex was encouraged by none other than Daniel O'Connell, a parishioner residing in nearby Merrion Square (see **24**). Both chapel and railway terminus were erected during the early 1830s, introducing a distinctive public character to what had previously been a private residential street. Residents in 1847 included music professors and esteemed men of medicine, mostly connected with the adjacent University of Dublin (see **28**). Most prominent of these was Sir William Wilde, surgeon to St Mark's Ophthalmic Hospital and father of the dramatist Oscar. A few doors south of the chapel at no. 40 was Robert Bell's Royal Baths.

Fig. 23: Dublin and Kingstown Railway (Westland Row), Cumberland Street, 1834, by J.D. Jones (NLI).

23. WESTLAND ROW

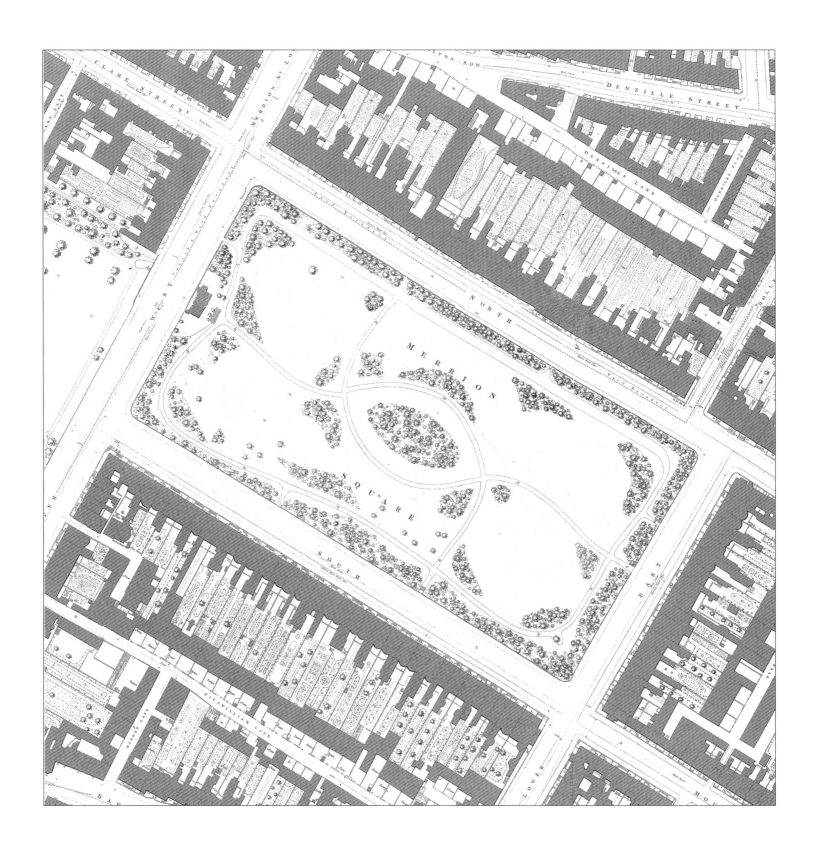

In 1797 the agent for the Pembroke estate, Barbara Verschoyle, in a letter to Viscount Fitzwilliam wrote: 'you have nothing in London so handsome as Merrion Square – the irregularity of the ground forms a first part of its beauty'. Indeed this aspect of the square was commented on by others. In 1818 George Newenham Wright observed that 'the great inequality of this area adds much to its picturesque appearance', while in the same year Warburton, Whitelaw and Walsh noted that 'Instead of reducing its surface, as usual to a perfect level, the person who planned the improvements has suited his decorations to the natural form of the surface, and thus at once produced a pleasing variety'. To the credit of the Ordnance Survey, even this aspect of the square is depicted on the 1847 map by the presence of contour lines, visibly absent on the flatter-surfaced St Stephen's Green (see **26**, Fig. 24, below).

The square was laid out in the 1760s and was the centrepiece of the Fitzwilliam estate. In terms of size, Merrion Square was the second

Fig. 24: West view of Merrion Square, including Leinster House and Clare Street, from *Hibernian Magazine*, 1801 (private collection).

square in the city after St Stephen's Green. In terms of status it was second to none and remained the most sought-after address in Dublin throughout the nineteenth century. Surrounded to the north, south and east by three unbroken terraces of lofty red-bricked dwellings, the

west side fronted the lawns of Leinster House, the most prestigious residence in the city (see **27**). Fitzwilliam had himself insisted on unbroken terraces in an attempt to maintain uniformity and continuity. The only exception was one carriage arch in the centre of the north terrace, which was filled in with a new narrow house in the nineteenth century, some time prior to 1843. Unlike the dwellings on the east and south terraces of plain red brick, the houses comprising the north terrace display a rusticated stone finish on the ground floor. The wide spacious carriageways and flagged pavements, particularly on the north side, became in the summer evenings 'the resort of all that is elegant and fashionable'. That the city's Great Exhibition of Art and Industry was staged on Leinster Lawn at the west end of the square in 1853 befitted the elevated status that this address retained into the mid-nineteenth century.

Residents of Merrion Square in 1847 represented the cream of the city's legal, medical and political circles. On the east side the Right Honourable Thomas Berry Cusack Smith resided at no. 8. During his time as attorney general for Ireland, 1842–6, Smith prosecuted Daniel O'Connell, who also lived on the square at this time. A few doors up at no. 11 – the present Irish Architectural Archive – Sir Thomas Staples, a prominent and wealthy lawyer, had his home. Their neighbour at no. 12 was James Benjamin Ball, principal partner in his father's banking firm, Ball & Co., located on Henry Street (see **13**). In 1842 he was elected a life member of the Royal Dublin Society (see **27**), one of his two proposers being his next-door neighbour, Henry Kemmis of no. 13 who was vice-president of the Dublin Society 1836–57. Next door at no. 14 was Sir Timothy O'Brien MP. O'Brien had made his wealth as a successful merchant, but went on to greater things by being elected lord mayor of Dublin on two separate occasions, 1844–5 and 1849–50. On the north side such eminent men of medicine as William Stokes, Sir Philip Crampton and Sir Henry Marsh resided within a few doors of one another.

24. MERRION SQUARE AND RESIDENTS

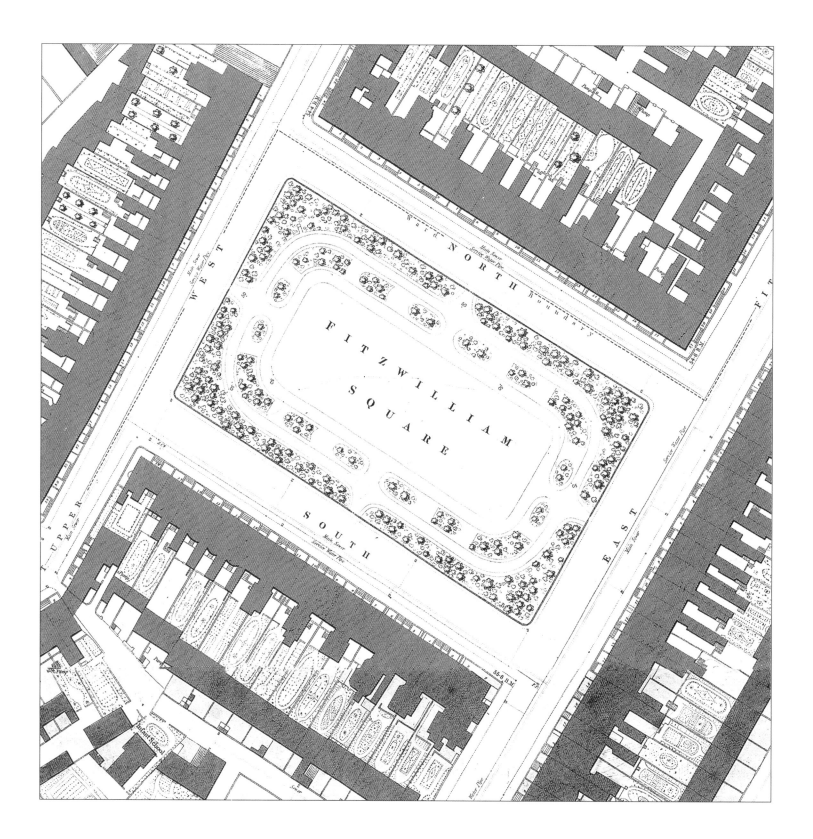

A few blocks south of Merrion Square (see **24**) stands its smaller neighbour, Fitzwilliam Square. Although laid out in 1791 and leases granted in the same year, building on this new square was very slow owing to concern over the approaching Union of 1801 and its possible impact on the housing market in this part of the city. By 1797 only four houses had been built on the north side and by 1806 only four more. The west side was developed between 1807 and 1815. However, it was the period after the Napoleonic Wars between 1816 and 1828 when real progress was made with the development of the east and south sides completing the square. Early concerns over the forthcoming Union were also reflected in the style of the houses being built. With four storeys over basement and two bays, these were smaller and of a less extravagant style than the houses on Merrion Square in order to suit the pockets of professional rather than aristocratic occupants.

The accompanying extract shows a well-kept garden surrounded by four terraces of houses, with railings to the front and spacious gardens and stabling to the rear approached by a stable lane. The garden square was surrounded by railings mounted on a dwarf granite wall with entrances at the mid-point of each of its four sides. The square was well-lit in the evening time, with fourteen lamps evenly distributed along the perimeter railings and a further fourteen outside the houses on each of the four sides. Remarkably, the gravel walkways and perimeter planting shown on the 1847 map are still in place today, the square having remained in private hands since 1813 when an act of parliament established fourteen commissioners from among the residents to look after and maintain it. During the 1840s and 1850s the garden matured significantly with tulips, crocuses and snowdrops planted in the flowerbeds and new trees and shrubs added along the perimeter walkways. Many scented plants such as sweet pea and stock were added during this period, thus enhancing further the impact of the garden in the summer evenings. Though in later years the grass lawn in the centre of the square was to be used for tennis, in the early years no sporting activity, including archery and croquet, was permitted by its commissioners, nor were dogs allowed in the garden.

In 1847 residents on the square included some of the city's most successful and influential professionals. On the south side at nos 1 and 9 were Nathaniel Hone (of the famous painting family) and Thomas Crosthwait respectively. The Hone and Crosthwait families were well connected; indeed not only were Nathaniel and Thomas brothers-in-law – the former having married the latter's sister – but so also had Nathaniel's two brothers married two more of Thomas's sisters. As was so often the case in such circles, family ties and business went hand in hand and Nathaniel acted as broker for Thomas's merchant firm. Thomas also sat on the board of commissioners for the square in 1862. On the north side of the square lived Pierce Mahony, one of the city's most eminent solicitors. The name of Latouche was still in this period connected with the square, the family having been represented on the original board of commissioners in 1813. Many of these houses in 1847 were occupied by gentlemen representing the higher echelons of the legal profession. On Fitzwilliam Place South, just south of the square, resided none other than Richard Griffith, responsible for the Geological Survey and Valuation of Ireland among many other professional achievements.

25. FITZWILLIAM SQUARE AND RESIDENTS

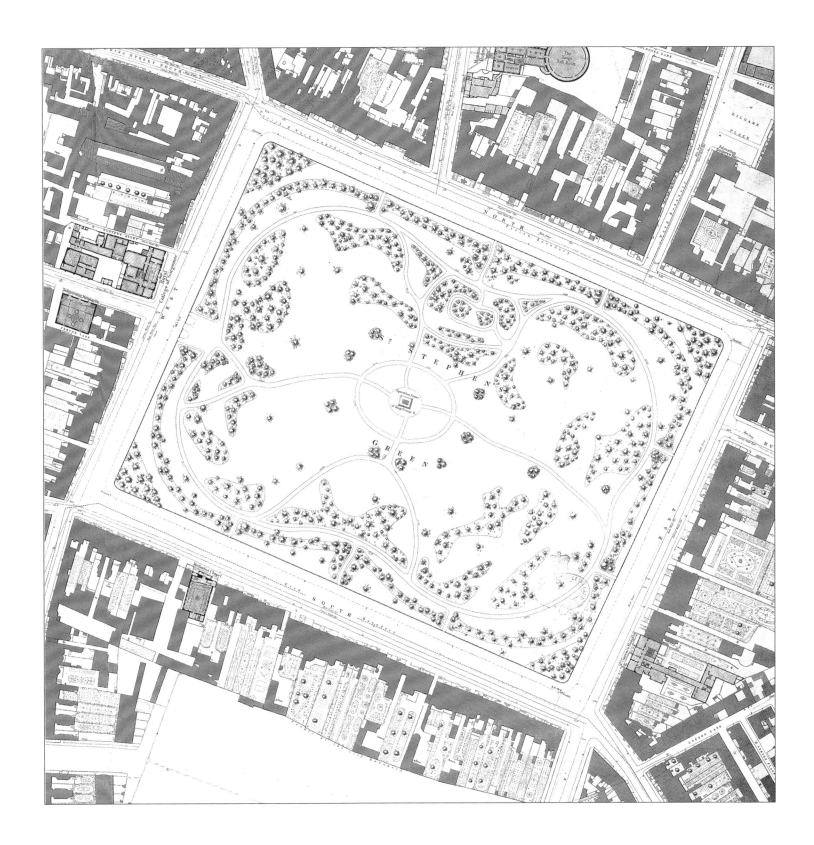

St Stephen's Green is the oldest of Dublin's public squares, laid out in 1664 on common grazing land. Charles Brooking's map of 1728 shows some vacant lots on the south side with the three remaining sides fully developed, a view that contrasts with that of John Rocque, who depicts the east side as the least developed in 1756. In 1678 a line of hedging was planted around the interior green, outside which was a ditch. On the outer side of the ditch a gravel walk lined by rows of tall elm trees adorned all four sides. Surrounding the gravel walk was a four-foot wall. Known locally as the Beau Walk, this walkway was a main attraction for the younger generations who used it frequently on Sunday evenings to promenade and show off their finery (Fig. 25, right). By the early nineteenth century the green had fallen into a state of neglect and a group of commissioners was appointed in 1815 to manage its improvement. The commissioners obliged by having the green levelled and planted with flowers. The ditch was filled in, the large trees cut down to allow light into the interior, and the wall replaced with a series of small stone pillars connected by iron chains. Within the gravel walk a dwarf granite wall surmounted by iron railings enclosed the green. An equestrian statue of King George II by Van Nost adorned the centre and is shown on the map extract and in the accompanying illustration (Fig. 25, right).

In 1847 the terraces surrounding the green were mostly of mid-eighteenth-century stock. On the west side is the Royal College of Surgeons, designed by Edward Parke in 1805. This building, still standing today, was easily the most striking on the green in 1847. The college was founded in 1784 and located close by in Mercer Street attached to the existing hospital. Very soon the college outgrew its original premises and in 1806 the present building at the corner of York Street was erected on the former site of a Quaker burial ground. The building was extended in 1825 to twice the original size and a new façade erected presenting onto the green. Contained within the new college were meeting rooms, lecture and dissecting rooms, a library and a museum. On the south side of the green stood a Methodist chapel (now the Department of Justice and Equality). The building stands two storeys in height with a portico of four columns. Opposition from the congregation of the Methodist chapel to the siting of the Dublin, Wicklow and Wexford Railway terminus next to the chapel resulted in the construction of that terminus farther south in Harcourt Street.

Situated on the east side was the original St Vincent's Hospital. The hospital was established by Mother Mary Aikenhead and the Religious Sisters of Charity with the object of looking after the sick

Fig. 25: St Stephen's Green, 1796, by James Malton (NLI).

poor of the city. The founders acquired no. 56, the former home of the earl of Meath (see **37**), in 1834 and the hospital was established the same year. All the properties on the east side of the green stand on a parcel of land that formerly belonged to the Blue Coat Hospital (see **2**). The original boundary of this land can still be made out in the unusual line of properties running in a north-easterly direction from Leeson Lane. At nos 8 and 9 St Stephen's Green North were the Hibernian United Service Club and Stephen's Green Club respectively, unnamed on the map, the latter with its racket court to the rear.

26. ST STEPHEN'S GREEN

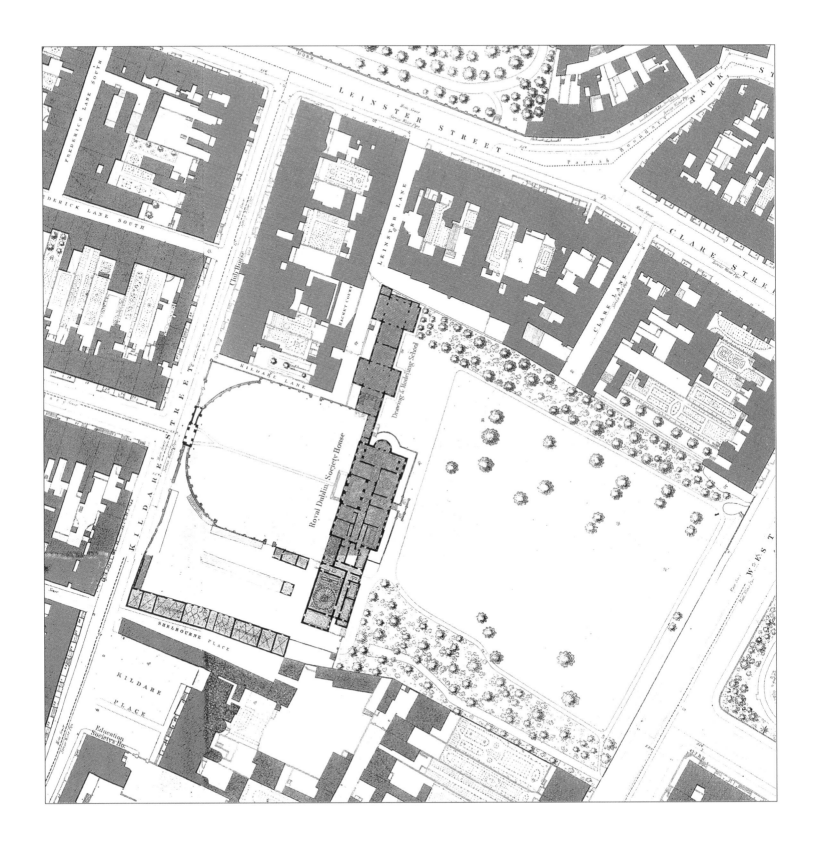

Not dissimilar to today, Kildare Street in 1847 was dominated by the presence of Leinster House. In 1815 the magnificent town house of the duke of Leinster had been purchased by the Dublin Society and became known as Royal Dublin Society House, as marked on the 1847 map. This extract captures the old Kildare Street about fifteen years before it had been remodelled to its more familiar layout today, with the Royal College of Physicians and the Kildare Street Club taking commanding positions on the east side of the north section of the street as far as Leinster Street. The Kildare Street Club had been formed in 1782 and named after the street where its premises were located. The house, built for the MP Sir Henry Cavendish, is marked on the map as 'Club House' and was well fitted out for a gentlemen's club with a card room, coffee room, reading room and billiard room. To the rear of the building and shown on the map was a racket court. By the late 1850s the club, with over 600 members, had outgrown its premises and the decision was taken to build a new home farther down the street on the corner of Kildare and Leinster Streets. This landmark building still survives today as part of the National Library of Ireland and the Alliance Française. Although not completed until 1861, the club was forced to move into its new home in 1860 when the original house, along with its library of 15,000 books, was destroyed by fire. The Royal College of Physicians built in 1862 now occupies the site of the former Club House.

The centrepiece of the street is Leinster House (Fig. 26, below left), the former home of James Fitzgerald, duke of Leinster and 20th earl of Kildare, hence Kildare and Leinster Streets and Lanes. Fitzgerald chose the underdeveloped Molesworth Fields district to locate his new town house, confident that his presence would attract fashionable development in the area. He was not wrong and within a few decades numerous new streets of first-class housing were laid out and many of the city's leading families moved to the area. The house was built in 1745 to a design by Richard Castle, the leading architect of the day. That Fitzgerald chose such an eminent professional is testimony to the importance and prestige that he attached to the project. The house is large in scale with three storeys and eleven bays. Neo-classical in style, four Corinthian columns separate and frame the three central bays, rising to a grand pediment with balustrades defining the ground and first floors above the front entrance. The Drawing and Modelling School formed the north wing of the main house and was approached via Kildare Lane, which now forms the entrance to the National Library of Ireland. A large lawn stretched out in front of the main building as far as Kildare Street with a narrow, straight pathway leading to the front entrance. To the rear of the house, the extensive Leinster Lawn rolled out as far as Merrion Square (see 24) and within six years of the publication of the map would provide the site of the Dublin Exhibition of 1853. Indeed the 1850s and 1860s was a period of great cultural development for this part of the city as the National Library, Museum and Art Gallery were all built on the Leinster House site.

Fig. 26: Leinster House, 1792, from James Malton, *A picturesque and descriptive view of the city of Dublin* (London, 1792–9).

27. KILDARE STREET AND LEINSTER HOUSE

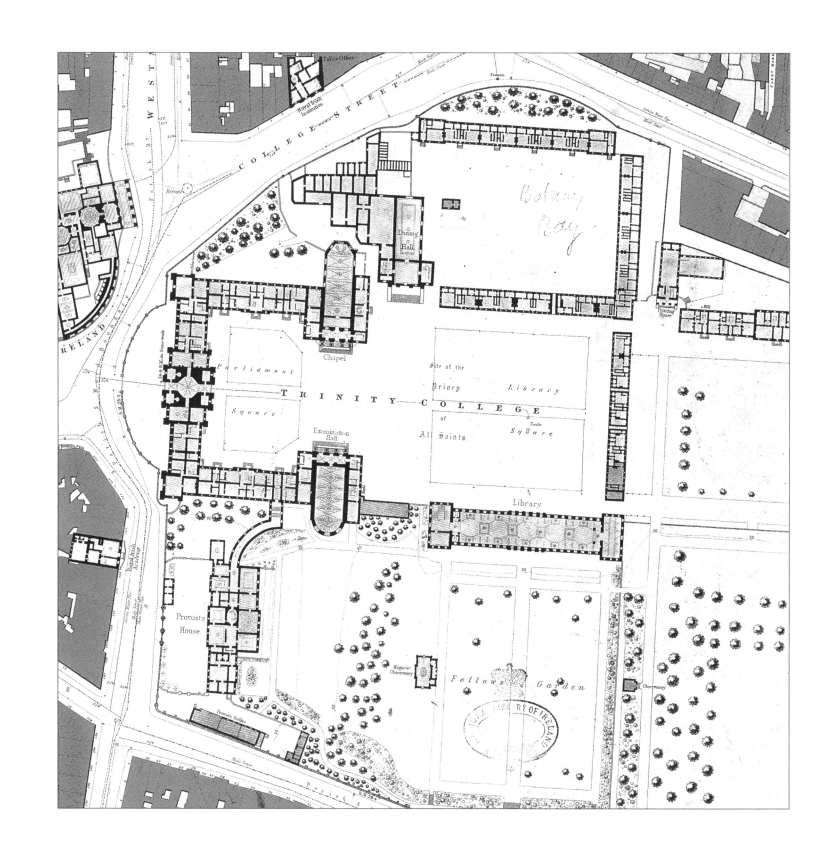

Trinity College occupies a commanding site in the heart of the Wide Streets Commissioners' newly-planned city. The re-modelling of the Parliament House and College Green and the linking of Westmoreland and D'Olier Streets with Sackville Street Lower via the new bridge (see **29**, **30**) shifted the dynamics of the city eastward. With Westland Row (see **23**) laid out since 1773 forming the eastern boundary of the site and the even longer-established Nassau Street bounding the college to the south, the laying out of Great Brunswick Street in 1812 defined the island site with its ensemble of neo-classical eighteenth-century architecture and College Park. The buildings are set around two main squares – Parliament Square to the west and Library Square to the east. Directly north of Library Square is an unnamed square, the present Botany Bay, formerly the site of a physic (botanical) garden, hence the name.

The west front presenting onto College Green stands four storeys in height and twenty-one bays across (Fig. 27, below left). Construction began in 1752 to a design by Theodore Jacobsen. An advanced seven-bay centrepiece with four Corinthian columns supports a grand pediment and entablature above the three central bays. Entrance is gained through a large archway above which a *piano nobile* forms the central bay. Two ranges on east–west axes join the building at right-angles on its north and south ends to form Parliament Square. The north range terminates with the chapel and the south with the ex-amination hall. Both buildings, designed by Sir William Chambers, face each other across the square with matching classical fronts. North-east of the chapel is the dining hall designed by Hugh Darley in 1760, and east of the examination hall the library building forms the south range of Library Square. The old library by Thomas Burgh (1712–32) is grand in scale and interior, the centrepiece of which is the Long Room. South of the library were the fellows' gardens laid out with gravel walks and lawns, from which students were strictly excluded.

South-west of the examination hall is the Provost's House (Fig. 28, below right) facing onto Grafton Street behind a high wall and gate. To the front of the house a courtyard provided access to a fine set of stables on the south wall at Nassau Street. To the rear, neat walkways, lawns and shrubberies offered a pleasant retreat for the provost and his guests. The house was designed for Francis Andrews, who was elected provost in 1758. The plan by John Smith was based on the house of General Wade in Mayfair, London, designed by Lord Burlington in 1723. The house is connected to the south range of Parliament Square through a narrow curved corridor from its north elevation. A scattered spread of evergreens across the lawn separated the main house from the fellows' gardens. Also depicted on the map is the magnetic observatory, the first to be built in the British Isles. Opposite the Provost's House at 114 Grafton Street was Navigation House, the original home of the Royal Irish Academy.

Fig. 27: Trinity College and College Green, 1795, from James Malton, *A picturesque and descriptive view of the city of Dublin* (London, 1792–9).

Fig. 28: Trinity College and Provost's House, 1794, from James Malton, *A picturesque and descriptive view of the city of Dublin* (London, 1792–9).

28. TRINITY COLLEGE AND PROVOST'S HOUSE

The construction of Carlisle Bridge in 1791 was of central importance to the social and commercial development of Dublin in the following century. The story of the bridge is closely tied up with the controversial re-siting of the Custom House from its old location upstream on Essex Quay to its present site on Custom House Quay (see **16, 17**). With exclusive residential development on the eastern edge of the city north and south of the Liffey, a new bridge upriver was required to link these fashionable quarters. Because the new bridge would close the old port to sea-going vessels, it would be necessary to relocate the Custom House east of the new bridge. Despite a determined stance by the powerful mercantile body to resist such a move, the even more powerful aristocrats won the day. The foundation stone of the new Custom House was laid in 1781 and in the following year parliamentary approval was granted for the new bridge.

Carlisle Bridge, named after the lord lieutenant, Frederick Howard, 5th earl of Carlisle, was completed in 1795 (Fig. 29, right). The bridge as shown in the extract was only forty feet wide and it was not until almost a century later that it was widened to suit the needs of the growing traffic. The design, by James Gandon, was of three semicircular arches of granite with a slight gradient towards the centre. On each side were balustrades of Portland stone. The location and style of the bridge paid tribute to the architect's masterpiece, the new Custom House farther downstream, with views said to be the finest in the city. Two public lavatories marked 'Retreat' are depicted on the map directly north and south of the bridge. That to the north on Sackville Street Lower was removed later in the century to make way for the O'Connell monument, while the larger convenience south of the bridge was moved farther east to Burgh Quay to accommodate the increasing traffic.

The bridge linked Sackville Street Lower to Dame Street and the Fitzwilliam estate via two new and broad streets, Westmoreland Street and D'Olier Street. On the east side of D'Olier Street was the Leinster Market, named Leinster Meat Market on the Ordnance Survey 1843 manuscript map of the city. Here customers could buy meat, poultry, vegetables and fish. Two doors from the market was the Dublin Library. This building, by George Papworth (see **14, 17, 32**), was erected specifically to house the collections of the Dublin Library Society which, since its formation in 1791, had been located in various premises in the city before moving to D'Olier Street in 1820.

East of D'Olier Street, on Hawkins Street, was the Theatre Royal built on the former site of the Dublin Society's house, which for some time had been the temporary home of the Mendicity Institution (see **40**). The building was destroyed by fire in 1880,

Fig. 29: Carlisle Bridge and River Liffey, looking west, *c.* 1850 (private collection).

rebuilt, then later demolished. The interior in 1825 was of extravagant Greek revival design with panels, gilt mouldings and frescoes on the ceiling dedicated to figures in Greek mythology. Directly north of the theatre was the Corn Exchange, a handsome two-storey building presenting onto Burgh Quay. The building was five bays across the front with two large entrance doors surrounded by pillars of Portland stone. Inside, a great hall 130 feet in length was the focal point of the building. Six metal pillars ran the length of the hall on either side, behind which were tables set out for the buying and selling of corn on market days. The large rooms to the front were used for public dinners and assemblies.

29. CARLISLE BRIDGE

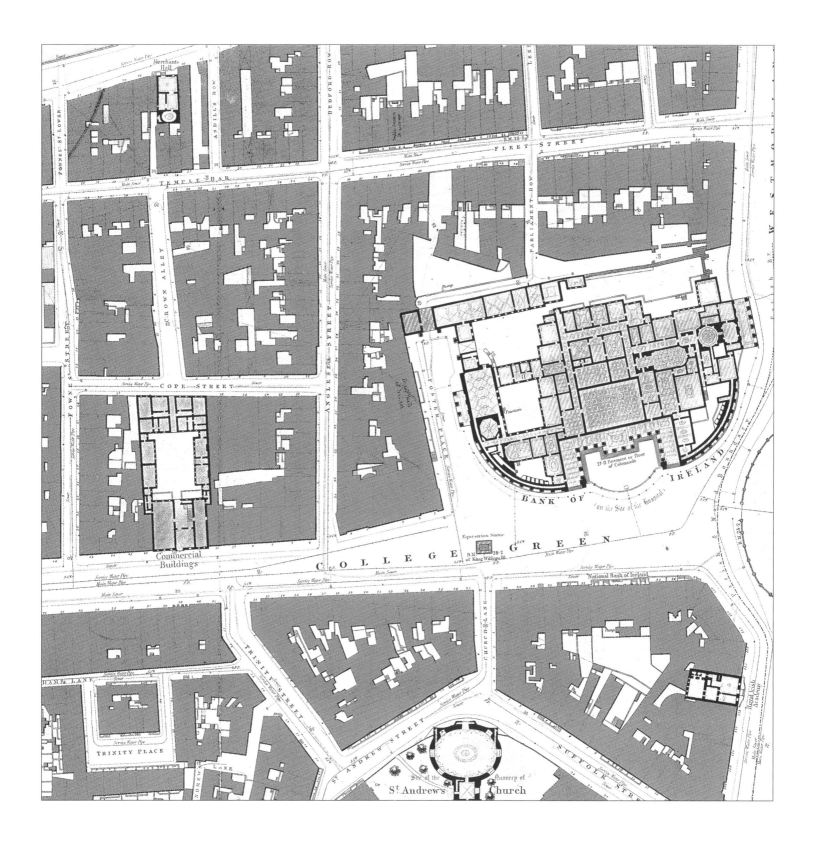

The purchase by the Bank of Ireland of the old parliament building in 1802 had repercussions for the surrounding district, with Commercial Buildings and the Royal Exchange already nearby in Dame Street (see **31**). The change of focus from political to financial became even more apparent after 1825 when new banking legislation paved the way for joint-stock banks. The National Bank of Ireland is shown on the 1847 map directly opposite the Bank of Ireland building at no. 34 College Green. The Royal Bank of Ireland, established in 1836 by Quaker capital, is also shown, though difficult to read, at Foster Place. Not identified are the numerous insurance agents', stockbrokers' and solicitors' offices that together with the larger institutions helped to make Dame Street, from Great George's Street South to College Green, the financial centre of the mid-nineteenth-century city.

The Bank of Ireland building as it stood in 1847 represented the work of numerous architects, three of whom were associated with eighteenth-century Dublin's most prestigious public buildings. The first stage of the building was the work of Edward Lovett Pearce begun in 1729. Pearce's colonnaded piazza is judged by Christine Casey to be 'the most powerful and original classical design ever realized in Ireland'. With the granting of parliamentary independence in 1782 it was decided to extend the building with a new east wing and grand entrance to the House of Lords. This work was begun by James Gandon in 1785 and was complemented by the Wide Streets Commissioners with the addition of Westmoreland Street and Carlisle Bridge linking the Parliament House to Sackville Street and the north city (see **29**, Fig. 30, below). The western extension to Foster Place was

the work of Robert Parke, carried out after 1787. Both extensions, with their curved screen walls, conceal all but the grand piazza of Pearce's original building. In 1804 Francis Johnston was assigned the task of converting what had been a parliament building into a bank. The fine detail of the 1847 map shows Johnston's significant reworking of Pearce's original interior. The wonderful Commons Chamber was dismantled and replaced by five separate compartments. Directly in front of this was Johnston's cash office, an amalgamation of the former Court of Requests and the Commons vestibule. The cash office and Upper House are still in place today.

Located just west of the Bank of Ireland along Dame Street was Commercial Buildings, another important financial institution in this part of the city. The Commercial Buildings Company was established by the city's prominent merchants in 1796 and opened for business in 1799. Its purpose was the day-to-day transaction of wholesale mercantile business, rather than the purchasing of bills that was the reserve of the Royal Exchange. The building with its internal courtyard is shown clearly on the map and takes centre stage among lesser buildings on the short block between Fownes Street and Anglesea Street. Rear access via the courtyard communicated with Crown Alley and the Metal Bridge. The design by Edward Parkes was an astylar elevation of three storeys and seven bays in golden granite. The building, which no longer survives, housed the Marine Insurance Company, the Stock Exchange, a hotel and coffee room in addition to a merchants' private subscription room and other ancillary offices. The Dublin Chamber of Commerce also had its early beginnings in this building.

Fig. 30: Bank of Ireland and Trinity College, College Green, *c.* 1875, from *Nelson's pictorial guide book for tourists* (London, 1875–80).

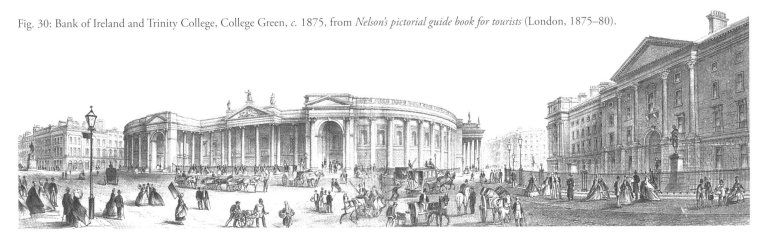

30. COLLEGE GREEN

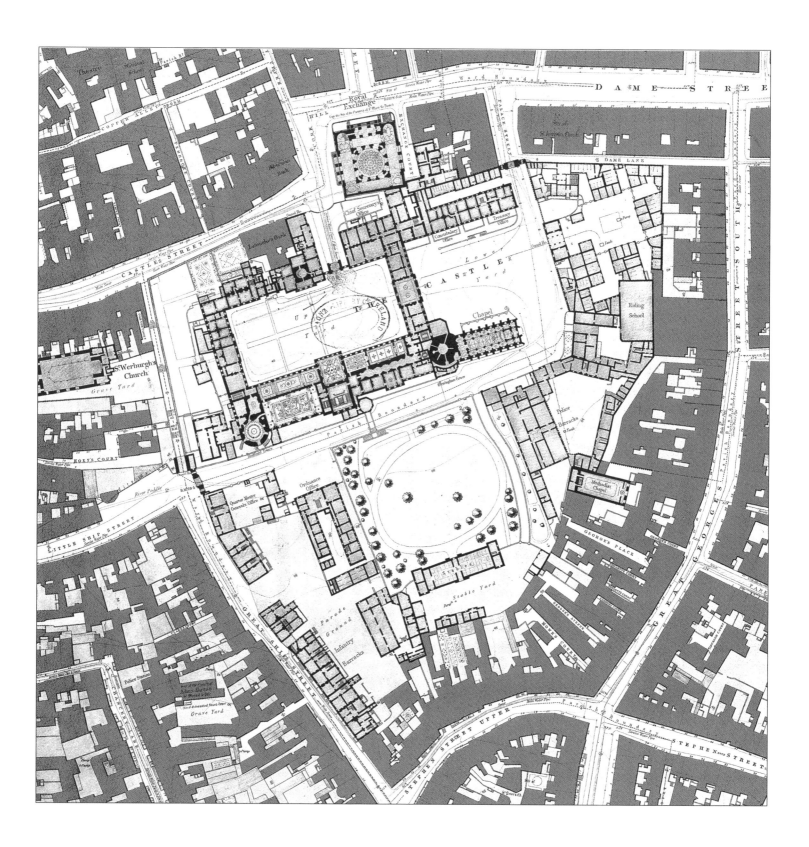

The heart-like enclosure of the Dublin Castle site, bounded to the north by Dame Street and Castle Street, to the west by Great Ship Street, to the south by Stephen Street Upper and to the east by Great George's Street South, has changed little, if at all, from John Rocque's *Exact survey* of 1756. Within these street boundaries, however, substantial change is evident by 1847, particularly towards the south-west corner where the residential character of Great Ship Street has all but been sacrificed with private houses remodelled into infantry barracks and other associated new buildings. The military aspect of this corner is emphasised by the additional presence of the Quarter Master General's office and the ordnance office, both substantial buildings that together with the infantry barracks surround a small parade ground. A well-known error on this particular sheet is the naming of the Bedford and Bermingham Towers, the reverse being correct with the Bermingham located in the south-west corner next to the magnificent St Patrick's Hall.

The piecemeal and somewhat haphazard development of the castle complex has been criticised by various commentators for its visible lack of planning. Nevertheless a closer inspection of the layout does disclose a co-ordinated plan. The entire complex can be divided into two sections. The original set of buildings centred around the Upper and Lower Yards to the north catered for the administrative and ceremonial functions of the castle, while to the south the newer buildings situated on either side of the spacious garden emphasised the castle as a site of defence and security. On the east side of the garden were situated the large police barracks, while directly opposite on the west side was the military complex. Located conveniently between both was the new stable building and stable yard, abutting the garden to the rear of the properties on Stephen Street Upper. Outside the castle compound a Methodist chapel can be seen immediately south-east of the police barracks and embedded in the rear of the housing on Great George's Street South. The chapel was opened in 1820.

When the Wide Streets Commissioners began their long-term project of street widening in the city, their first scheme was the laying out of Parliament Street in 1757. This involved removing the old Cork House and adjoining Lucas Coffee House, creating a large open area on Cork Hill and thus providing a long uninterrupted vista from the castle entrance down the new street to Essex Bridge and Capel Street beyond. In 1768 the cleared ground was given over to the Merchants' Exchange Trustees for a fee of £4,000. The money required to build the exchange came from subscriptions and lotteries and a parliamentary grant of £13,500. The Merchants' Exchange, or Royal Exchange as it came to be known, was designed by Thomas Cooley and represented one of the most advanced neo-classical buildings in the country at the time (Fig. 31, left). It was completed in 1779 at a cost of £58,000. Shortly after the publication of the town plan of 1847, the building ceased to be used as the Royal Exchange and was purchased by Dublin Corporation and thereafter served as the City Hall. Outside the main entrance next to the guard house was Latouche's Bank and opposite on the corner of Cork Hill and Castle Street stood Newcomen's Bank.

Fig. 31: Royal Exchange, 1792, by James Malton (NLI).

31. DUBLIN CASTLE AND ROYAL EXCHANGE

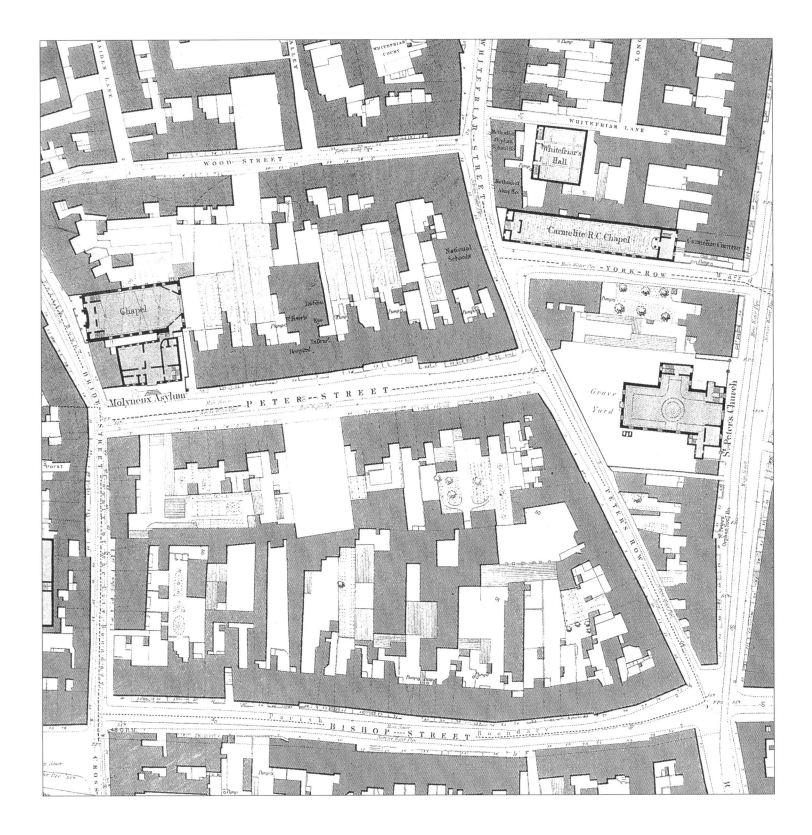

The tightly compacted area enclosed between Bride Street and Aungier Street in the parish of St Bridget, and bounded by Wood Street and Whitefriar Lane to the north and Peter Street and Peter Row to the south, contains an unusually high concentration of religious, medical and charitable institutions. On the north corner of Bride Street and Peter Street stood the Molyneux Asylum and Chapel. The institution was established for the care of blind females and in 1815 acquired Molyneux House on Peter Street, the former mansion of Thomas Molyneux, as its permanent home. The house was built in 1711 and had remained in the hands of the Molyneux family until the 1780s when it was taken over by Philip Astley, an English equestrian performer and circus proprietor, who built a theatre to the rear of the house in 1789. Astley's Royal Amphitheatre of Horsemanship opened in 1789 and remained a popular form of entertainment for the citizens of Dublin until its closure in 1815 following Astley's death. On acquiring the premises in 1815, the asylum committee fitted out the house to accommodate fifty blind females, while the amphitheatre to the rear was converted to an asylum chapel, similar to the way in which the Smock Alley Theatre had been converted to St Michael and St John's Catholic Chapel on Essex Street Lower.

About six doors east of the asylum, St Peter's Hospital and the Dublin Eye Infirmary stood next to each other. St Peter's Hospital, formerly known as St Peter's and St Bridget's Hospital, was founded in 1810 by John Kirby of the Royal College of Surgeons for the sick and needy of the two parishes (see **26**). The hospital included a lecture theatre in which Kirby and other medical practitioners gave lectures. In the street directory for 1847 this building and the Dublin Eye Infirmary are listed as the Dublin School of Medicine and Surgery, and Anglesey Lying-in Hospital. At the east end of Peter Street were a national school and farther south on Aungier Street were St Peter's Church and graveyard and Orphan Society House.

The Carmelite R.C. Chapel on Whitefriar Street and York Row still stands today, though the orientation has been reversed. In 1847 the front entrance stood at the west end of the church on Whitefriar Street, with the convent to the rear where the present front entrance and vestibule now stand. The church was designed by George Papworth (see **14**, **17**, **29**) between 1825 and 1827 and was extended in 1844 and in 1859. Immediately north of the church was Whitefriar's Hall on the site of the former eighteenth-century meeting house of the Methodist Missionary Society. The Methodist connection remained in 1847 with the Methodist Orphan School House and Methodist Alms House sited west of the hall on Whitefriar Street. The almshouse was erected in 1766 for poor and infirm widows in the district in need of subsistence. Twenty widows were 'comfortably accommodated' with beds, bedding, coal, candles and a small amount of money per week. Attached to the house was the orphan schoolhouse for boys and girls of all denominations.

32. ST BRIDGET'S PARISH

The wonderful Portobello Gardens on the South Circular Road were one of the city's greatest treasures and their disappearance in 1865 one of its great losses. In the summer months the gardens were open from ten o'clock to dusk. Adults were admitted for six pence and children under ten for half price. All manner of fantastical entertainments drew the public to these exquisite landscaped gardens throughout the year, including in winter time when ice skating took place on the frozen man-made lake. Vast crowds of 'beauty, rank and fashion' thronged to the gardens to witness the variety of exhibitions on offer, including a demonstration of the destruction of the cities of Pompeii and Herculaneum by the eruption of Mount Vesuvius. This bizarre display was re-enacted on a weekly basis during the summer of 1840 with a mound from which emanated mimic fires to the sounds of rolling thunder. This was preceded by instrumental concerts and the appearance of a lion tamer with his caged beasts. On 13 May 1847 the *Dublin Evening Post* announced the opening of a newly-erected concert hall within the gardens. The hall, on an 'extensive scale', provided entertainments for many.

Contemporary newspapers describe the vast array of exotic animals on display including a Bengal tiger, Asiatic leopard, kangaroos, vultures, eagles and cockatoos. In 1850 Mr Gomez, professor of archery, displayed his skills to all. During this period the gardens, then being referred to as the Royal Portobello Gardens, were described as the 'Vauxhall of Dublin'. Nevertheless the alternative description, the 'Palace of cheap amusements', may suggest that they were already on the decline at this point. In August that year, the flying man appeared to the thrill of many, descending a rope sixty feet high and 300 feet across the gardens surrounded by 'gold and silver fire'. Novel equestrian acts followed, topped by Signor Lupino's performing dogs. In 1855 John Clarke begged to inform the nobility, gentry and the public that he had become the new lessee of the gardens and intended to render them fashionable again as in 'days of yore'. In 1859 a licence had been granted for the sale of wines in the gardens, as acts became even more daring with Mr Talleen walking on the waters of the lake, balloon ascents, trapeze, aquatic sports and the rather less daring, yet curious, 'intelligent dogs'.

Fig. 32: Grand Canal and Portobello Bridge, *c.* 1820, by S.F. Brocas (NLI).

The gardens are depicted in all their magnificence on the Ordnance Survey map with shrubberies, picturesque walkways, a music hall unnamed in the centre and two lakes at the northern and southern ends. Of note is the gasometer depicted in the north-west corner, necessary for the frequent pyrotechnical displays. In 1862 the gardens fell victim to an arson attack and were closed. For three years they lay neglected and in 1865 their future was sealed with a decision by Dublin Corporation to grant permission to Frederick Stokes, the main developer of Rathmines and Portobello, to drain the lands and cover them with houses. Today the former site of the gardens is occupied by Stokes's housing development, Kingsland Park and Victoria Street. Despite its name, the New City Basin shown immediately east of the gardens had been in place since 1806. Parke Neville, the City Engineer (1851–86), had designed a small waterworks on the fifth lock of the Grand Canal (Fig. 32, above) for breweries and distilleries in the area; this may help to explain the presence of the 'distillery water pipe' shown on the map (see **34**).

33. PORTOBELLO GARDENS

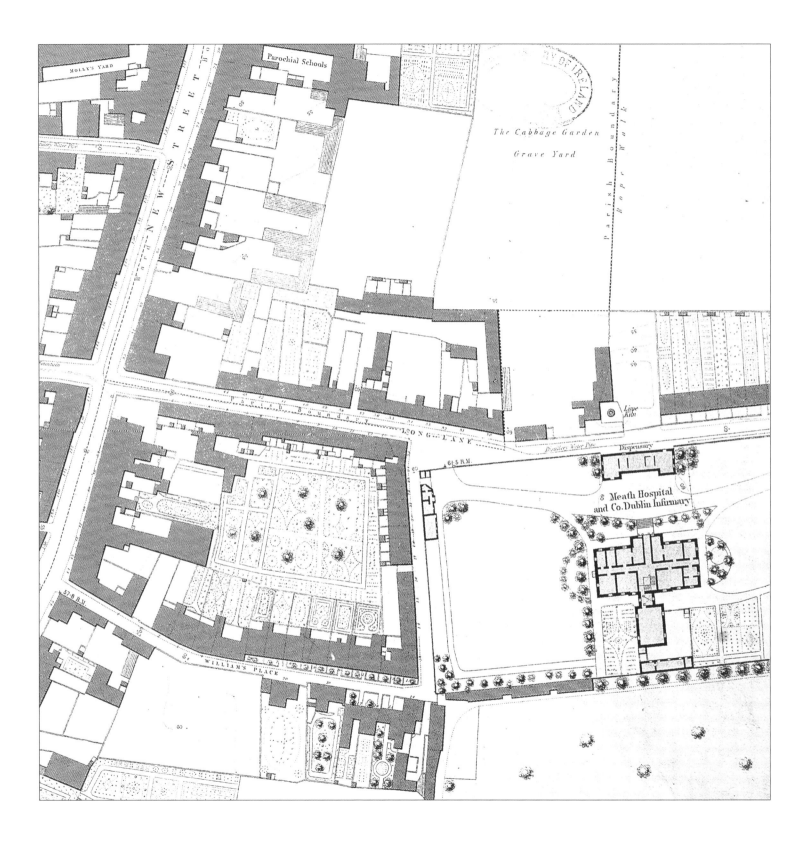

The Meath Hospital and County Dublin Infirmary was built in 1822 on the plot that Dean Swift referred to in 1749 as Naboth's Vineyard. The history of this institution dates back to 1753 when a hospital was founded for poor people living in the earl of Meath's liberty. The original hospital started out on Meath Street before funds permitted the construction of a new and larger building in The Coombe. The new Coombe building was opened in 1773 and in the following year, under an act of parliament, the hospital became the Meath Hospital and County Dublin Infirmary (Fig. 33, right). With this added responsibility the building in The Coombe became inadequate and a larger premises was once again required. The present site on Heytesbury Street was purchased in 1815 with the help of a generous donation of £4,000 made by Thomas Pleasants. Pleasants, a wealthy merchant and philanthropist, donated significant sums of money towards the poor of the Liberties and it is fitting that his name is commemorated in the street situated south-west of the hospital in the extract. The new site chosen was that of Dean Swift's former vineyard on the south side of Long Lane. Although not an actual vineyard, the dean had used this garden to cultivate fruit and it may be significant that an orchard is shown directly south of the hospital on the 1847 map.

The building shown in the extract still stands today as part of the complex known as the Meath Community Service, the Meath and Adelaide Hospitals having been incorporated into Tallaght Hospital in 1998. The building stands three storeys over a tall basement and is nine bays wide, comprising three bays on either side of a three-bay central projection crowned by a pediment. This central projection is visible on the map. Like many of the institutional buildings of this period, the stone used in the exterior is calp rubble. Directly north of the front porch, along the south-facing perimeter wall where the dean's peach, nectarine, pear and apple trees once blossomed, stood the dispensary. Two gates on the east and west side of the complex permitted entrance to the hospital from Long Lane. The main building was set back in extensive lawns with walkways, shrubs and flowerbeds to the rear. An interesting feature in this extract is the distillery water pipe shown running past the hospital on Long Lane from the New City Basin in Portobello to John Busby's distillery on Fumbally Lane (see **33**). North of the dispensary was the southern tip of the Cabbage Garden graveyard, used in the early nineteenth century to relieve pressure on the crowded St Patrick's Cathedral churchyard.

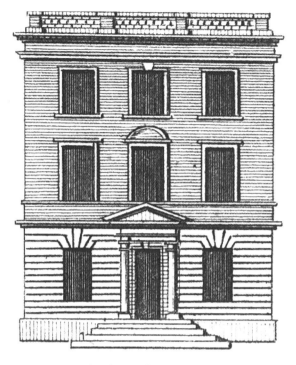

Fig. 33: Meath Infirmary, from *Gentleman's Magazine*, May 1786 (private collection).

34. MEATH HOSPITAL

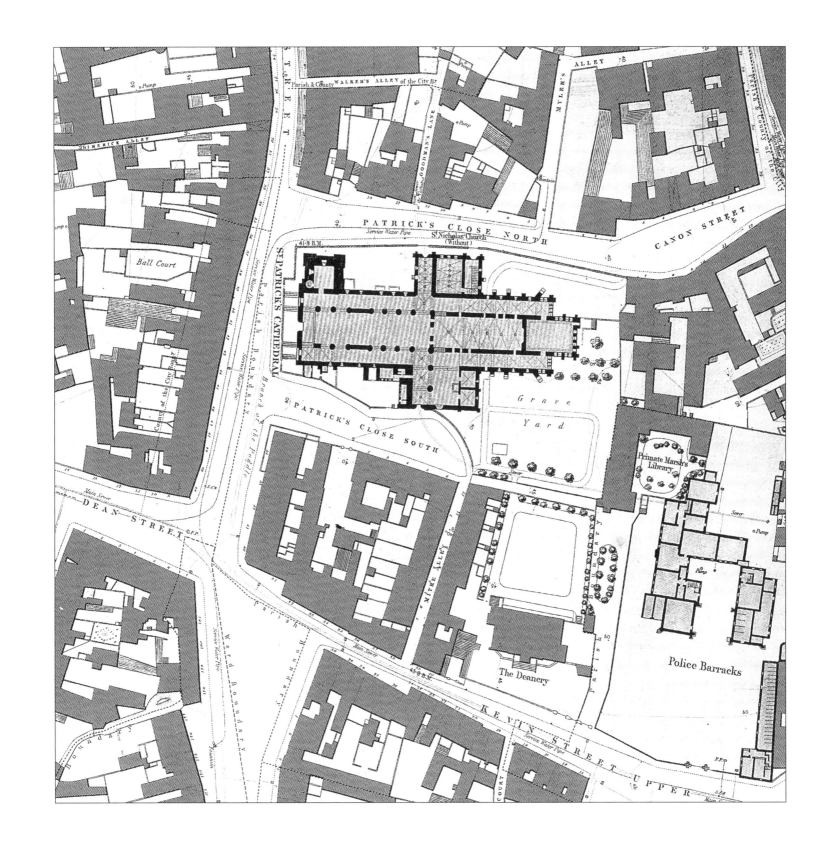

The 1847 map captures St Patrick's Cathedral just before it underwent its massive late nineteenth-century overhaul (Fig. 34, right). At the beginning of this century the cathedral, like nearby Christ Church, had fallen into serious disrepair. In 1805 it had even been recommended for demolition. Although the basic structure looks little changed from John Rocque's period, substantial reworking had taken place by 1847. The north transept, in use since the thirteenth century as the parish church of St Nicholas Without, was still serving the same function in 1847, access being gained from St Patrick's Close North. Houses abutting the north-eastern end of the building had been removed by 1847 and St Patrick's Close North extended eastwards in the form of Canon Street, following the route of the narrower Petty Canon Alley before opening onto Bride Street. On the south side of the cathedral the graveyard visible on Rocque's map remains, separating the south-eastern end of the building from Primate Marsh's Library. As demand for plots increased, a new graveyard had been opened south of Kevin Street for burials (see **34**). Buildings had also been removed from the south-western end, while to the front of the cathedral the widening of Patrick Street had resulted in the removal of further housing. While not discounting these 1840s improvements, much of the exterior we see today dates from the 1860s renovation by Benjamin Lee Guinness.

The low-lying ground upon which the cathedral was built was prone to flooding in extreme weather. This problem was exacerbated by the River Poddle flowing only centimetres below street level across the cathedral's front entrance. For this reason an efficient system of drainage was necessary. The extract shows a network of drains north and south of the cathedral connecting to the underground Poddle. Also shown are a series of grates at street level providing an outlet into which the excess water flowed. A main sewer is shown running beneath the north and south transepts into the dense housing north of the cathedral. This housing surrounding Walker's Alley, Goodman's Lane and Myler's Alley was one of the worst slums in the nineteenth-century city and was removed in the later part of the century to make

Fig. 34: St Patrick's Cathedral, *c*. 1850 (private collection).

way for the present St Patrick's Park. The building of this park in 1903 required the removal of St Patrick's Close North and Canon Street.

Primate Marsh's Library south-east of the cathedral was built between 1701 and 1703 and was extended in 1710 by Thomas Burgh. Marsh had been provost of Trinity College before becoming archbishop of Dublin. In this latter role he opened his library 'for publick use' where all could have free access to important works of literature. The most notable feature of this building today is its interior with its original book cases. In the extract, a ball court is shown to the rear of nos 38 and 39 Patrick Street. Such amenities were viewed as a social nuisance since they attracted the idle. This particular court was located to the rear of a tinplate workshop through which access was gained.

35. ST PATRICK'S CATHEDRAL

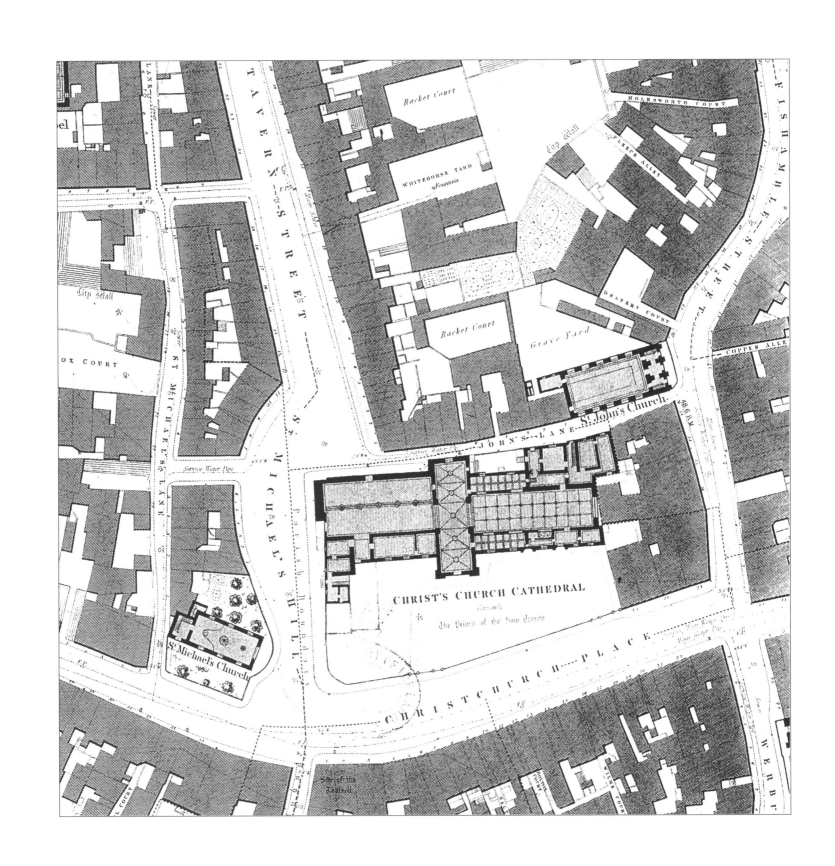

For more than a century down to the 1820s, Christ Church Cathedral, formerly the Priory of the Holy Trinity, had been hidden from view by a dense pile of ramshackle buildings concealing the main edifice on its south, east and west sides. In 1818 Warburton, Whitelaw and Walsh commented on the cathedral's exterior, 'disfigured and disgraced by the mean habitations ... pressed against' its walls. The narrow cramped streetscape depicted on Rocque's *Exact survey* of 1756 shows the cathedral, as it remained until 1818, before the enactment of the Wide Streets Commissioners' improvement scheme for the area (Fig. 35, right). The new improvements replaced the existing streets and lanes with broad thoroughfares and in the process removed much decayed housing in the immediate vicinity. On completion of the scheme the ancient cathedral re-emerged from among the decrepit housing that had cloaked its exterior for centuries. Here the Ordnance Survey 1847 map is

Fig. 35: Winetavern Street, Christ Church, *c.* 1820, from Thomas Cromwell, *The Irish tourist* (London, 1820).

crucially important since it provides the first finely detailed cartographic record of the Wide Streets Commissioners' improvements to the city between 1757 and 1847. The accompanying extract shows the replacement of the older narrow streetscape with a spacious open plan. Skinner Row and Christ Church Lane had been replaced by Christchurch Place and St Michael's Hill, the latter sweeping past the cathedral's western entrance to join up with the newly-widened Winetavern Street north of the cathedral.

The 1847 map also provides one of the last cartographic depictions of the medieval cathedral before its massive nineteenth-century overhaul. This later refurbishment, funded by the distiller Henry Roe in the 1870s (see **39**), involved the construction of the Synod Hall on the site of St Michael's Church south-west of the cathedral. The new hall was joined to the main building by a covered arched walkway over St Michael's Hill, thus creating one of the city's most iconic landmarks. At the opposite north-eastern end of the cathedral stood

St John's Church, Fishamble Street, closed in 1878 when the parish merged with St Werburgh's. Immediately west of the graveyard adjoining St John's was one of a number of racket courts sporadically located about the city. These early precursors of the modern tennis court were often associated with idleness and vice, and were usually located in the less salubrious parts of the city. This particular court was one of two at the back of the numerous inns and alehouses that formed the aptly-named Winetavern Street.

South of Christchurch Place on the corner of Nicholas Street is the site of the old tholsel, rebuilt in 1682 as a merchants' hall and serving the purpose of City Hall until it was demolished in 1820. On the façade of this grand building stood two carved wooden statues of Kings Charles II and James II, above which was a wooden royal coat of arms. These are the only surviving remnants of one of Dublin's most important civic buildings and are now on view in the crypt of the adjacent Christ Church Cathedral.

36. CHRISTCHURCH PLACE

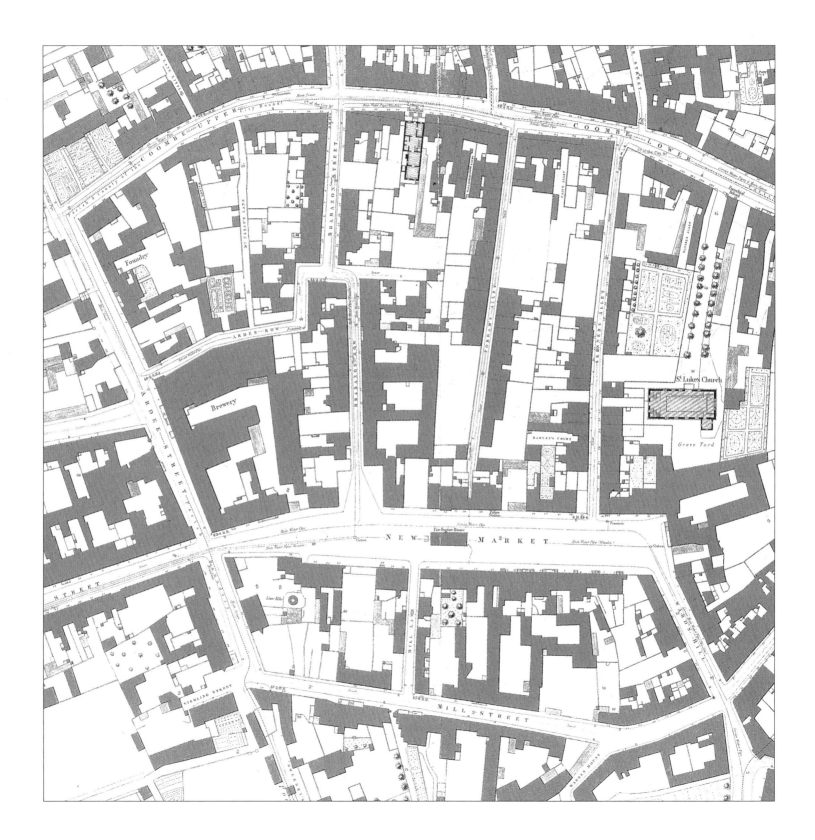

After the dissolution of the monasteries in the sixteenth century, the Liberty of St Thomas, the largest of Dublin's medieval Liberties, was granted to William Brabazon, earl of Meath. For a variety of reasons, not least of which was an abundant supply of fresh water, this area developed into one of the most industrialised parts of the city by the mid-nineteenth century. The process began in the seventeenth century and continued into the eighteenth, with Quaker and Huguenot communities settling in the area and establishing weaving and other textile industries. The presence of the River Poddle enabled the brewing and distilling industries to flourish as new streets were laid out in close proximity to its numerous tributaries. By the mid-nineteenth century the tanning industry was heavily concentrated in this tightly-knit district. The area shown in the extract within the boundaries of Coombe Upper and Lower, Ardee Street, Mill Street and Skinners Alley is a microcosm of the larger Liberties district, with weaving, brewing, distilling, tanning and milling much in evidence. Street names such as Brabazon Street and Row, Ardee Street and Meath Street commemorate the earls of Meath, while Mill Street, Skinners Alley and Weavers Square, the latter outside the bounds of the extract, reflect the types of activity prevalent in the area.

Situated on the south side of Coombe Lower, east of Brabazon Street, was the Coombe Lying-in Hospital. This building began life as the Meath Hospital and County Dublin Infirmary (see **34**). When the latter moved to new premises on Long Lane in 1819, the vacant building was reopened as the new Coombe Lying-in Hospital. In 1836 the hospital was capable of accommodating thirty-four patients and gratuitously attended to an average of 100 out-patients a day, the majority of whom were the local poor. The hospital afforded training opportunities for young doctors under leading practitioners such as Drs Cheyne and Kirby (see **32**), consulting physician and surgeon at the time who, in addition to treating patients, delivered lectures on midwifery and diseases of women and children. There was also a dispensary from which medical staff attended patients in their homes. The building, now demolished, consisted of three storeys over a basement and eight bays with a two-bay central projection and quoined brickwork. The front porch depicted on the map was an elaborate affair of four columns with a central arch supporting a pediment. Sadly the porch is all that remains of the building today.

The extensive breweries of Richard and Joseph Watkins are depicted on both sides of Ardee Street at nos 10 and 11 on the east side and 22 on the west side. Though previously affluent, by the mid-nineteenth century the Liberties had become associated with poverty. In 1847 all but two of twenty-nine properties on Skinners Alley were tenements and by 1884 the site north of Coombe Upper between Pimlico and Meath Street became the first of Dublin Corporation's nineteenth-century slum clearance schemes, as the Dublin Artisans' Dwellings Company replaced the demolished slums with new brick dwellings. Also of note in this extract is the wide open space of Newmarket, with the Fire Engine House in the centre still serviced by wooden water pipes. Although Dublin Corporation had by 1809 begun the long process of replacing all wooden pipes with metal, the Liberties fell outside the jurisdiction of the corporation and therefore retained its older wooden pipes until later in the century. South of Newmarket (once again outside the boundaries of the extract) was a Carmelite convent, the former Warrenmount House and mills, once home to Nathaniel Warren, lord mayor of Dublin in 1782–3. The Carmelite nuns acquired the house in 1813 and in 1892 it was handed over to the Presentation sisters. The house survives today as part of the Warrenmount Presentation Convent.

37. THE LIBERTIES

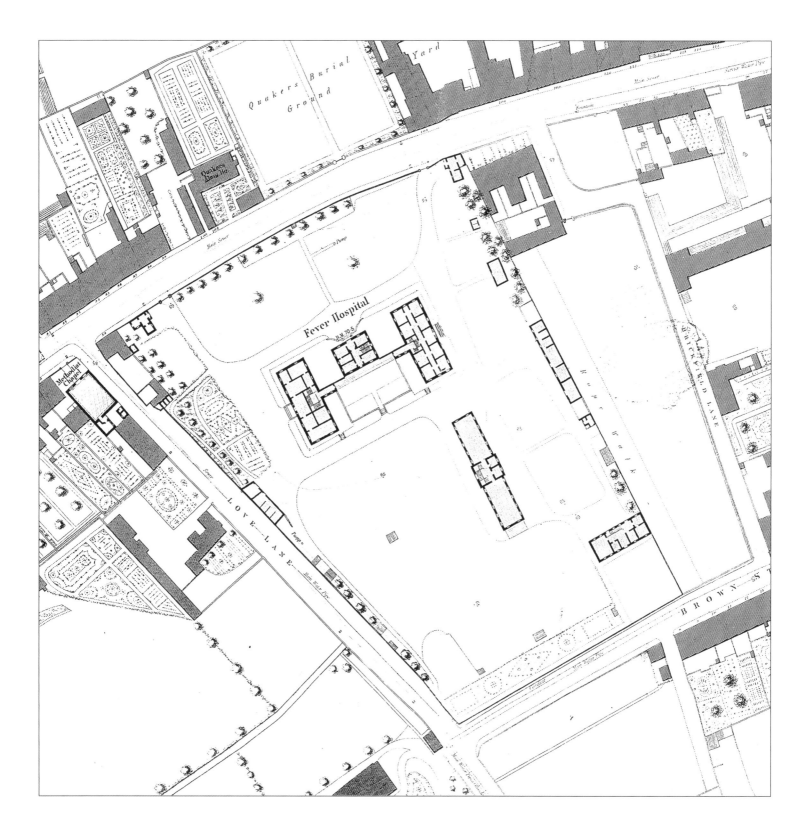

The Cork Street Fever Hospital was built between 1802 and 1808 on a three-acre site known as the Widow Donnelly's Orchard. Located on the south side of Cork Street, the rectangular site was bounded by Love Lane to the west, Brickfield Lane to the east and Brown Street to the south. Heightened awareness of the dangers of overcrowding and disease, particularly in the Liberties, led to a meeting in the Royal Exchange in 1801, the objective of which was to establish a house of recovery or fever hospital for the sick poor of that district. The hospital would cater for patients residing in the parishes of St James, St Catherine, St Audoen, St Luke and St Nicholas Without. In 1805 this remit was extended to take fever patients from all parts of the city south of the Liffey and within the Circular Road. Fifteen trustees from among the city's wealthy business class were elected and assigned the task of raising funds for the hospital. Among these men were representatives of the Guinness, Bewley and Latouche families. The site was chosen for its fresh air and plentiful supply of water; the Poddle and its many channels are shown on the map cutting through the fields in the immediate vicinity.

The map shows two blocks, one facing east, the other west, and both linked by a narrow corridor to a central north-facing block. The buildings, which survive today as a nursing home, are of yellow brick. The two outer blocks are of three storeys above a basement with windows on the east- and west-facing sides only. Both blocks were built between 1802 and 1804 and housed the patients' wards. The east block facing the city contained the fever wards, while the west block open to the fresh westerly breezes and country air contained the convalescent wards and officers' apartments, facing onto pretty landscaped gardens. Whitewashing was used in the fever wards since it was believed that lime helped to sanitise infected materials. This block shows nine separate, identical wards with a long corridor down the middle. Each ward contained three cast-iron beds. The convalescent wing was of a less geometric plan, the rooms within varying in size and shape. In the basement of this wing were the kitchen, scullery and morgue. The central block was completed a few years later in 1808 and contained apartments for new staff and yet more wards. Directly opposite the hospital was the Quakers' burial ground and almshouse. Immediately east of the almshouse, though unnamed on the map, was a widows' asylum set up by David Latouche, one of the fifteen trustees and one who contributed generously to the establishment of the hospital. On the corner of Love Lane and Cork Street was a Methodist chapel.

38. CORK STREET FEVER HOSPITAL

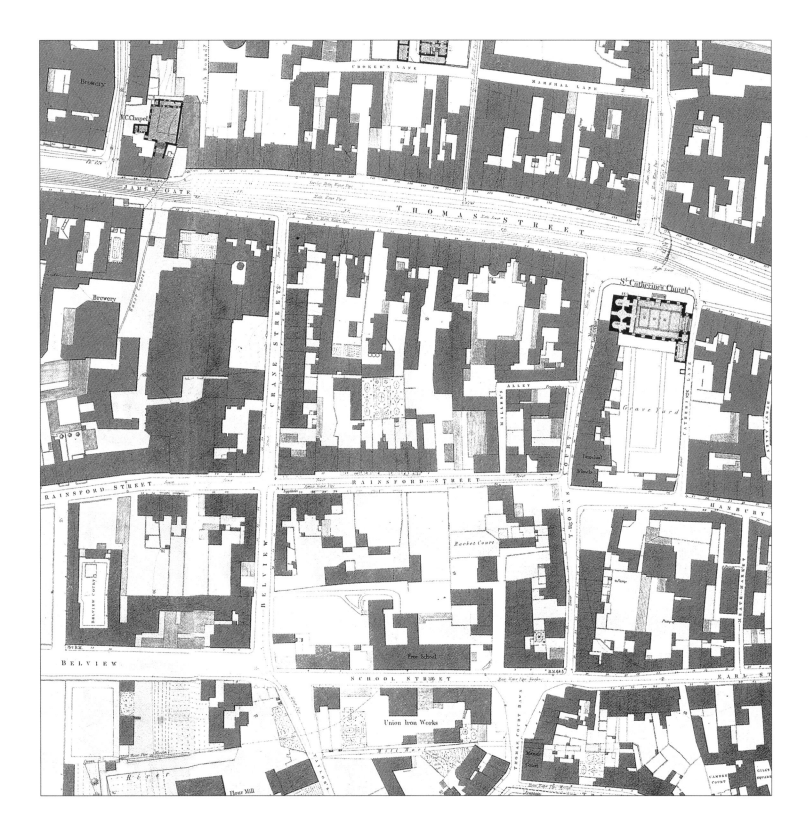

Dublin's industrial quarter in the mid-nineteenth century was located in the south-west corner of the city, dissected on an east–west axis by the thoroughfare comprising James' and Thomas Streets. A multitude of breweries, distilleries, mills and foundries occupied the back lanes and side streets on both sides of this dividing artery. The agricultural-based brewing, distilling and tanning industries were most plentiful in this part of the city, encouraged no doubt by the presence of the nearby Grand Canal and harbour with its direct links to the south-west hinterlands. The famous St James's Gate site of the Guinness brewery (labelled brewery and shown south of James Gate on the extract) had been in operation since 1670 when the original owner had secured rights for water from the corporation. The property, including the water rights, then passed into the hands of Mark Rainsford, an eminent brewer whose name is commemorated in the adjoining street. In 1759 Arthur Guinness acquired the title to the property and began building his celebrated company, which by 1847 was one of the largest in Ireland and the Guinness name well-known in Dublin society.

North of James Gate at the junction of Watling Street was the famous Phoenix Brewery owned in 1847 by Robert Cassidy. Cassidy had recently taken over this business from Daniel O'Connell junior, son of the Liberator. O'Connell junior had acquired the business in 1831 and began brewing his own O'Connell Ale on the premises. Directly opposite the entrance to Crane Street on Thomas Street was the arched entrance to Roe's distillery. George Roe opened his distillery in 1757, two years before the Guinness brewery was established. The Roe distillery grew to be one of the largest in the world before it was closed at the end of the nineteenth century. The generosity of George's relative, Henry Roe, in refurbishing Christ Church Cathedral in the 1870s has been mentioned as a factor in the financial failure of the company in the 1890s (see **36**, **40**). A large smock windmill known as St Patrick's Tower survives as a remnant of the old distillery. The windmill with its onion dome once ground corn for the distillery and is one of the street's more familiar landmarks today.

St Catherine's Church, Thomas Street, survives and stands on high ground at the top of Bridgefoot Street, terminating a long vista from Queen's Bridge and the river. In order to make maximum use of the site, the architect, John Smith, when designing the church in 1760–69, chose the north-facing side elevation as the architectural showpiece of the building. Four half columns and two pilasters support a large entablature and central pediment (Fig. 36, below). The elevation is broad with five bays and expressed from the exterior as two storeys with balustrades above the two outer bays. A large round-headed doorway forms the central bay flanked on either side by two round-headed windows above two flat segment-headed windows. To the rear of the church between Catherine Lane and the properties on Thomas Court was the graveyard. In 1835 the cemetery was almost disused, since the poor of the parish were by then interring their relatives in the country churchyards. Of note among the deceased was James Whitelaw, the vicar of St Catherine's, who died in 1813. Whitelaw, together with the historian, John Warburton, worked on an historic study of Dublin yet neither man lived to finish the task. In 1818 it was compleed and published by Robert Walsh as the *History of the city of Dublin*. South of the graveyard was Thomas Court Bawn, the original site of the abbey from which the Liberty of St Thomas derives its name. Immediately east of this historic site was the Union Iron Works and mill race.

Fig. 36: St Catherine's Church, Thomas Street, 1797, from James Malton, *A picturesque and descriptive view of the city of Dublin* (London, 1792–9).

39. WESTERN INDUSTRIAL QUARTER

At a meeting held in the Rotunda Rooms on 22 January 1818, the Association for the Prevention and Suppression of Mendicity in Dublin was established. Among the committee members was Thomas Pleasants, who provided much of the funding for the Meath Hospital (see **34**), members of the Bewley and Latouche families, and the lord mayor who was elected president. From rather humble beginnings in Hawkin's Street, the association eventually moved via Copper Alley to the vacant Moira House in 1823 (Fig. 37, below). Situated on Usher's Island, this was the former home of the earl of Moira, built in 1752. On taking ownership of the new premises, the association immediately began renovating them and in 1836 the *Dublin Penny Journal* reported: 'This once lordly mansion, has been so much altered to suit its present purposes, that we are unable to give a correct drawing of it'. The extract shows the Mendicity Institution and its surroundings in 1847, a period when street begging was at a height owing to the influx of paupers from the famine-ravished countryside. During this period the Mendicity Institution provided food and medical attention for up to 2,900 people a day.

Dependent beggars and those in need of subsistence were divided into categories by the institution. Many of the recipients were able-bodied adults and were employed in spinning, knitting, straw-plaiting and rug-making. For this they were paid an amount agreed by the committee to be fair. Others doing less valuable work such as street-sweeping and clothes-mending were paid a lower rate. Adults

Fig. 37: Moira House, by William Brocas, from *Hibernian Magazine*, 1811 (private collection).

considered to be infirm were fed, clothed and given lodgings. Children were divided into two categories, those over six and those under six. The former were 'educated and instructed in useful employment' with one meal a day; the latter were fed and cared for while their parents worked. The Poor Law Union Workhouse system, funded by the ratepayers, gradually superseded the Mendicity Institution but there were still those who preferred its day-time, non-residential character to submitting to the strictures of indoor relief.

Directly south of the Mendicity Institution, situated on the corner of Marshalsea Lane and Croker's Lane, was the Four Courts Marshalsea. The building was entirely of limestone and the east wall along Marshalsea Lane was completely without windows. Compared to the grim conditions in the City Marshalsea in Green Street (see **8**), those confined in the Four Courts Marshalsea enjoyed relative luxury. The main building was designed around two courtyards. The south courtyard was said to have pumps in the centre that yielded a constant supply of fresh water. The yard to the north also contained a cold bath for prisoners. Neither of these is shown on the map. Accommodation was described in 1835 as 'tolerably good', with unnamed common halls and a ball court shown to the extreme north of the complex. The north-eastern perimeter wall still survives today as does the court. West of the marshalsea was the Roe distillery in Bonham Street (see **36**, **39**).

40. MENDICITY INSTITUTION

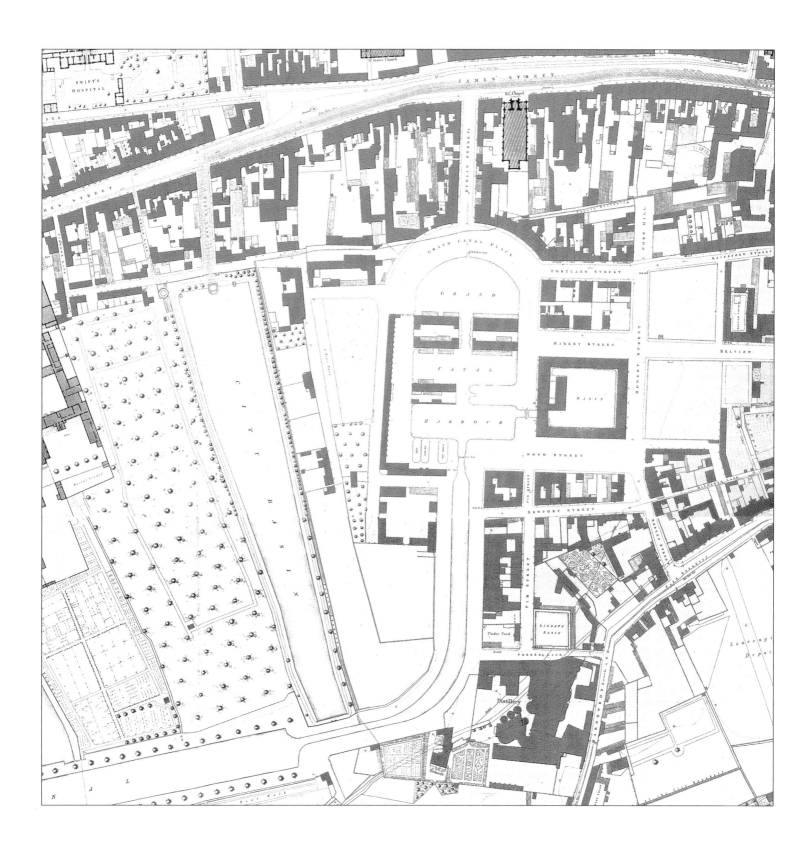

With such extensive industry in the south-west section of the city, particularly the large number of breweries and distilleries, it was important that a good supply of water was readily available. Not only were the brewing and distilling industries dependent on fresh water as an ingredient, water was also required for steam-powered machinery and for the transportation of goods. In this respect the City Basin at Basin Lane and the Grand Canal Harbour were both strategically placed to cater for the needs of this intensely industrialised part of the city (Fig. 38, right). The harbour at Grand Canal Place was built by the Grand Canal Company and completed in 1785 as the original terminus of the Grand Canal, the already existing City Basin and nearby Guinness brewery being determining factors in the location of the harbour. The canal route was extended by way of the circular line between 1790 and 1792 to link up with the Liffey at Ringsend. The new harbour connected the numerous industries in the James' Street and Thomas Street district with the remainder of the country and facilitated trade between the capital and the rural hinterlands. The harbour and adjoining warehouses were quite extensive, comprising two rectangular and one semicircular basin all interlinked. The south basin north-west of Bond Street also connected with three dry docks and a fourth larger basin east of the main harbour. West of the harbour a long unbroken range of buildings ran from north to south closing off access to the bonded warehouses and dry docks, which could be accessed only through two gateways at either end of the range. Within this range of buildings was a police station. North of the harbour the buildings on either side of Echlin Street followed the curve of the north basin to form Grand Canal Place, which opened onto the water. In 1863 the Guinness brewery built a new set of curved warehouses directly on the water's edge, part of which still survives today.

Fig. 38: City Basin and Grand Canal Harbour, extract from view of 'City of Dublin', from *Illustrated London News*, 1 June 1846 (private collection).

One of the main objectives in siting the harbour at James' Street was to provide a good supply of water for the existing City Basin. The basin, originally constructed in 1724, is shown on Charles Brooking's map of 1728 enclosed by a gated wall with a neat tree-lined walkway around the perimeter. In addition to providing the city with water, the basin also became another of the city's fashionable places of promenade in the late eighteenth century. The perimeter walkway was still in place in 1847, as shown on the map. This extract illustrates the usefulness of the Ordnance Survey's depiction of water mains and sewers. A high concentration of water mains can be seen leaving the basin at its northern tip and moving north along Basin Lane before turning east along James' Street. South of the basin the Cammock and Poddle rivers are shown flowing alongside each other, at which point the Poddle takes its subterranean route under the south-west city before entering the Liffey. The City Basin continued to be a main source of water for Dublin until the Vartry scheme came into operation in 1862.

41. GRAND CANAL HARBOUR

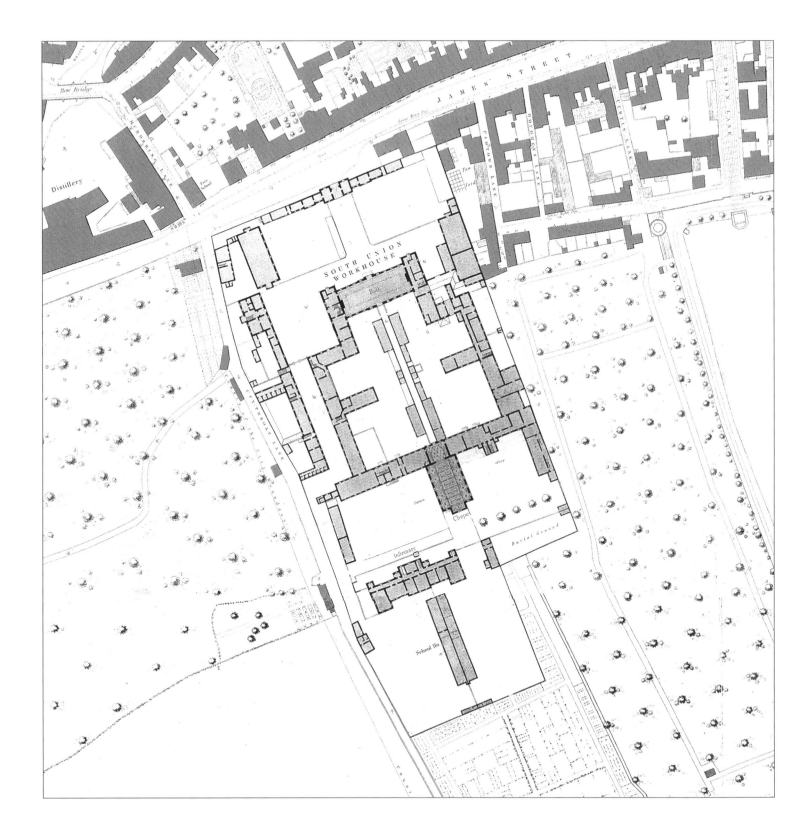

The South Union Workhouse represents a single phase in the long evolutionary process from City Poorhouse and foundling hospital to Union Workhouse and modern city hospital. Development began on the site in 1702 with the construction of a workhouse for the city's poor. In 1727 the workhouse building was extended and took on a new role as foundling hospital for abandoned children. The hospital admitted from 1,500 to 2,000 children annually from all parts of Ireland and even as far as Wales. In 1822 an act was passed stating that a deposit of £5 be made with each child so as to reduce the annual numbers being admitted to below 500. Hundreds and probably even thousands of children died within the walls of this institution until it closed its doors in 1837. That the workhouse originally included a bedlam and bridewell within the complex reflects how confinement was a routine response to mental illness, disability or petty offending among the poor. Depravity and desperation are conveyed in the local nomenclature, with Cut Throat Lane forming the western boundary of the complex and Murdering Lane on the opposite side of James' Street. West of the complex was Pigtown Lane. The extract shows the site in 1847, a decade after the passing of the Poor Law Ireland Act of 1838, which divided the country into 152 Poor Law Union districts. Each district had its own workhouse: the North Dublin Union workhouse occupied the former House of Industry site in Grangegorman (see 4), the South Dublin Union Workhouse the former foundling hospital at James' Street.

The Bridewell that was shown on Rocque's map at the north-east corner of the site on Mount Brown is still partly visible though not labelled on the 1847 Ordnance Survey map. Although the basic structure of the original workhouse and foundling hospital still survived in 1847, the new complex had by this time developed

Fig. 39: Dining hall, foundling hospital, 1817, from Warburton *et al.*, *History of the city of Dublin* (London, 1818).

considerably around the original buildings. The large dining hall (Fig. 39, above) was still in place with its eight round-headed windows designed to absorb as much light as was possible from the north-facing wall. In the mid-eighteenth century a linen factory and master's house were added to the ensemble on the west side of the main building. A chapel was also added on an east–west axis, but in 1803 Francis Johnston, having just remodelled the Parliament House into a bank, was called in to redesign the workhouse buildings. Johnston rebuilt the chapel in Gothick style on a north–south axis, thus bringing the east and west ranges of the former bedlam together as a single unit. South-west of the chapel he built a large detached infirmary and south of that a detached schoolhouse. East of the infirmary was a burial ground. By 1847 the street frontage had also been built up and numerous new buildings had been added on both sides of the site.

42. SOUTH DUBLIN UNION WORKHOUSE

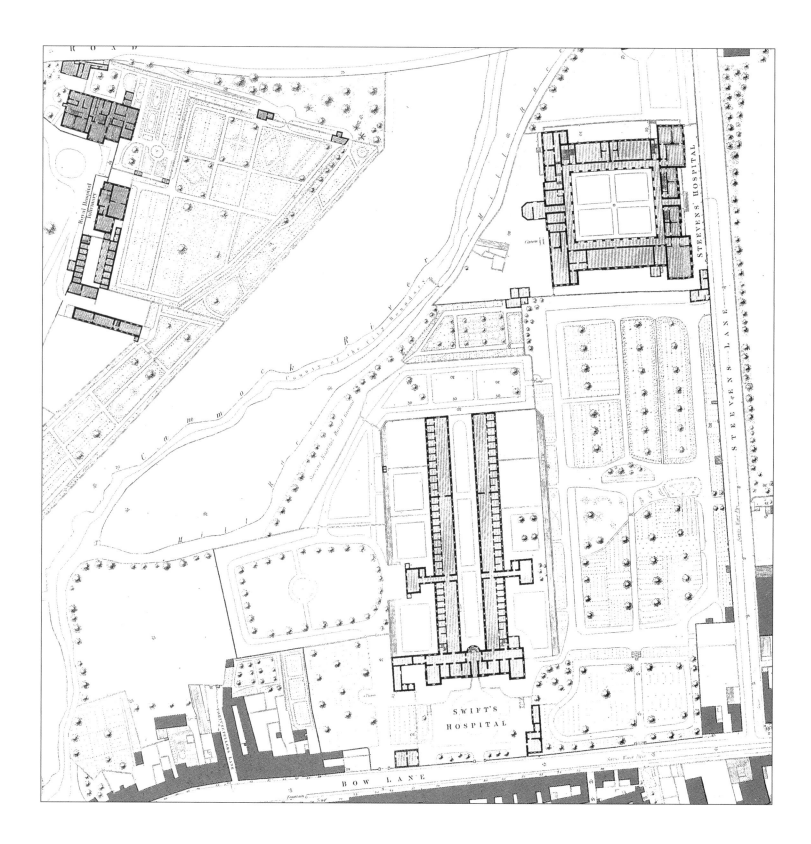

The Ordnance Survey map shows Dr Steevens' and Swift's Hospitals standing in close proximity to one another on a small triangular parcel of cultivated land bounded to the east by Steevens Lane, to the south by Bow Lane and to the north-west by the Cammock River. Dr Steevens', the first of the two to be built, was, like many of Dublin's hospitals, established under charitable auspices. On his death in 1710, Richard Steevens, a wealthy surgeon, bequeathed his estate to his twin sister Grizel for her lifetime, after which it was to be used to found a hospital for the sick poor of the city. Grizel, a benevolent spirit like her brother and anxious to fulfil his wishes, immediately set about appropriating what turned out to be insufficient funds to establish the hospital. Although building began in 1719, it was not completed until the mid-1730s, yet the hospital admitted its first patients in 1733. The building was designed by Thomas Burgh, one of the trustees of the hospital, along with Dean Swift and other esteemed figures in Dublin society. The plan is quadrangular, consisting of four two-storey fronts with dormer roof, enclosing a courtyard surrounded by a piazza with covered gallery. What was originally the main entrance on the east front, now closed to the public, is distinguished by a large cupola with bell and clock. The hospital's greatest treasure is the Worth Library: located in the north-eastern corner of the building, this contains the entire collection of Dr Edward Worth, surgeon and one of the original board members.

A wall running east to west from Steevens Lane to the Cammock River separated Steevens' from Swift's Hospital. The latter was founded at the behest of Jonathan Swift, who on his death in 1745 bequeathed his estate to the establishment of a hospital for the reception of 'idiots and lunatics', the terms used at the time to describe those suffering from mental illness. As a trustee of Steevens' Hospital, Swift stipulated in his will that the new hospital be built close to Steevens' and his wishes were followed. Swift's Hospital was erected on land acquired from the neighbouring hospital and laid out in a walled rectangular plot with its front entrance presenting onto Bow Lane. The original building, as shown on John Rocque's map, was a compact

U-shape with two wings running south to north at right-angles to the main edifice. Both wings, containing the ward ranges, were extended by Thomas Cooley in 1777 to a length of 327 feet. Each wing contained three wards with a corridor running the entire length, onto which the cells opened. A contemporary source describes 158 twelve-

Fig. 40: The Royal Hospital, 1766, from Walter Harris, *The history and antiquities of the city of Dublin* (Dublin, 1766).

by-eight-foot 'cells' in the two three-storey wings, sixty-two of which are visible on the 1847 map. The map also shows the newly-extended hospital set back from Bow Lane and surrounded by extensive gardens planted with trees and a spacious courtyard to the front. On the 1838 manuscript map a ball court is marked towards the south-east corner of Steevens Lane and Bow Lane.

Completing Dublin's south-west hospital quarter was the Royal Hospital (Fig. 40, above) located farther west on high ground overlooking the Liffey, with elaborate landscaped gardens to the front decorated with walkways and a fountain in the centre. This inspiring complex, standing at the end of an impressive tree-lined avenue entered through the Richmond Guard Tower, was begun in 1680 and developed in stages before being reworked in 1805 by Francis Johnston. The south-west hospital quarter was one of two hospital quarters in the city, the other comprising the House of Industry hospitals on Brunswick Street North (see **3**).

43. SOUTH-WEST HOSPITAL QUARTER

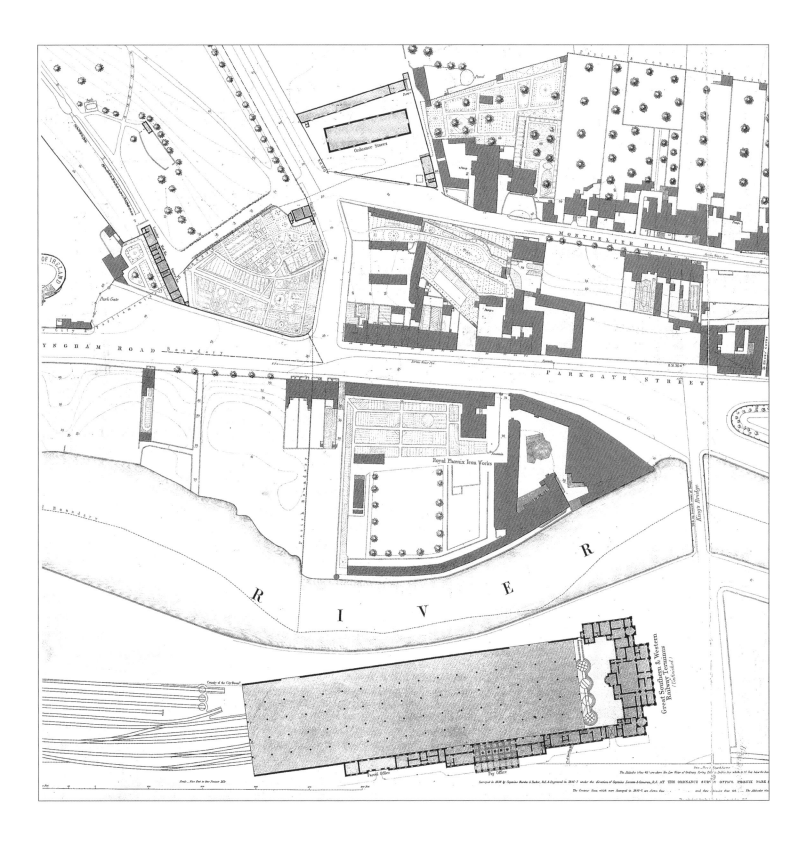

PARISH & COUNTY OF THE CITY

Ordnance Stores

MONTPELIER HILL

OF IRELAND

Park Gate

YNGHAM ROAD Boundary

PARKGATE STREET

B.M. 25.4

Boundary

Royal Phœnix Iron Works

King's Bridge

R I V E R

County of the City Bound.

Great Southern & Western
Railway Terminus
(Unfinished)

Parcel Office

Pay Office

Scale Five Feet to One Statute Mile

Surveyed in 1838 by Captains Hardee & Tucker, R.E. & Engraved in 1846-7 under the direction of Captains Larcom & Cameron, R.E. AT THE ORDNANCE SURVEY OFFICE PHŒNIX PARK

The Contour lines, which were Surveyed in 1846-7 are shown thus

The terminus of the Great Southern and Western Railway at King's Bridge is one of the most ornate buildings in the city and by far the most superior of the four railway termini. Situated, as was usual, on the edge of the city, the King's Bridge terminus was designed by Sancton Wood and completed in 1848. The large shed to the rear of the building was completed two years previously by the great railway engineer, Sir John MacNeill. The terminus was located conveniently to the Royal Barracks for the rapid dispatch of troops in times of emergency and was also close to the Guinness brewery. However, like the other termini in the city, King's Bridge was isolated from the wider city network and remained so until 1872 when the company built a tunnel under the Phoenix Park to link with the Midland Great Western Railway and, via the Liffey Junction Railway, to connect with the docks at the North Wall. The main building, two storeys in height, stands nine bays across its east-facing front. This impressive façade is flanked on either side by a single-storey wing surmounted by a domed campanile. The first-floor *piano nobile* is defined by ten engaged Corinthian columns supporting a balustrade, above which is a central five-bay attic. All nine windows are crowned with alternating pointed and round-headed pediments. Carved swags and urns decorate the five central bays in line with the attic above. The ground floor is of a rusticated design with the main entrance flanked on either side by two large arched entrances. The long low south elevation that contained the parcel office and pay office is of a less ornate design than the main east-facing façade.

Directly north of the terminus the Liffey flows on its easterly course towards Dublin Bay. The 1843 Ordnance Survey manuscript map shows the river with its natural banks on the south side before the construction of the western quay walls. South-west of the King's Bridge the Cammock is shown flowing through the future site of the terminus building. By 1847 the Liffey had been walled in with a new south quay replacing the old Military Road and leading directly to the front of the terminus and north to the King's Bridge. North of the railway terminus on the north side of the river was Richard Robinson's Royal Phoenix Iron Works. Robinson, a native of Hull in England, opened his iron works on this site early in the nineteenth century. The works was responsible for casting the nearby King's Bridge to commemorate the visit of King George IV in 1823 (Fig. 41, below). As a result the Phoenix Iron Works was given the prefix 'Royal' in its title. This building, which abuts the north bank of the river, still survives today.

Fig. 41: King's Bridge, 1831, by George Petrie, from *Dublin delineated in twenty-six views of the principal buildings* (Dublin, 1831).

44. KING'S BRIDGE RAILWAY TERMINUS

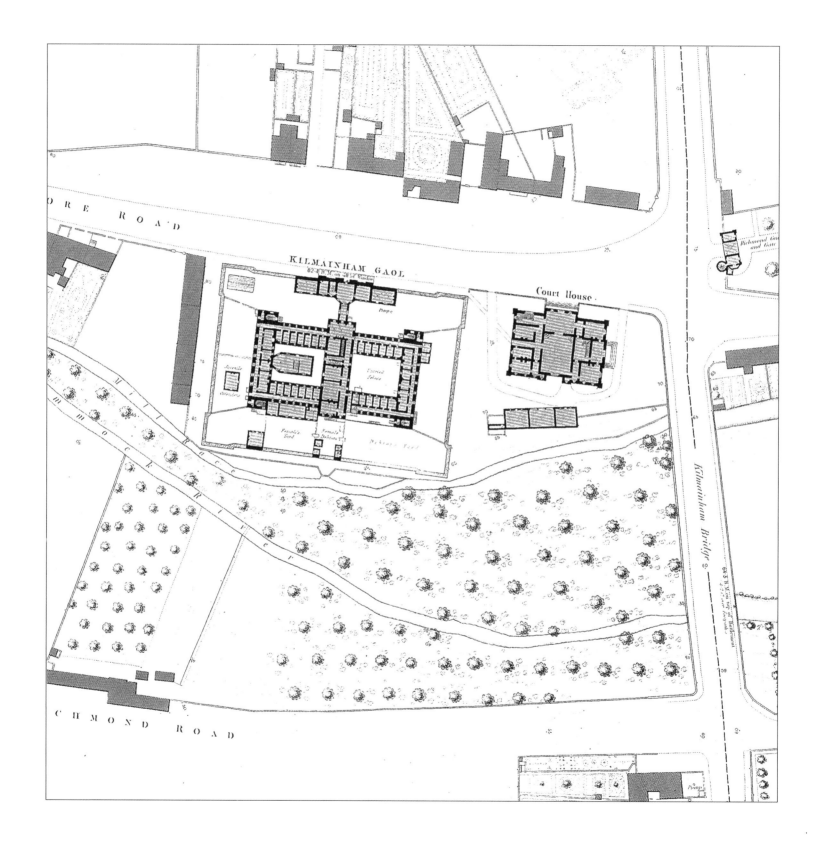

KILMAINHAM GAOL

Court House.

ORE ROAD

CHMOND ROAD

Richmond Guard
and Gate

Kilmainham Bridge

The County of Dublin Gaol at Kilmainham was opened in 1796 to replace a former gaol in Old Kilmainham. The prison was sited on high ground on the south side of Inchicore Road. To the rear of the complex the ground sloped down through a wooded area to the Cammock River and orchards on Richmond Road. As a place of confinement the rectangular site was enclosed within a high perimeter stone wall. A separate channel from the river formed a mill race, which passed eastwards along the south wall under Kilmainham Bridge towards the mills at Rowserstown. Within this wall were the yards for the separate classes of prisoner and in the centre the main prison building. In the south-east corner was the debtors' yard while to the south-west was a smaller yard for female prisoners. Juvenile offenders, some of whom were as young as eight years, were allocated a separate yard at the western end of the site, but in some cases were forced to share cramped cells with the adult prisoners. The prison building, which survives, is in a double quadrangular style with two inner courtyards, that to the east for the accommodation of 'untried felons'. On the north front of the complex a narrow corridor connects the front entrance on Inchicore Road with the main building. This corridor provided access to the warders' apartments and cells. Also located in the main building was a chapel in the west quadrangle, an infirmary, a common hall, and a workroom where female prisoners engaged in weaving and other handicrafts.

As the County Gaol, Kilmainham was the last place of detainment for all prisoners awaiting transportation, including those from the northern counties. In 1823 the inspectors general for prisons in Ireland reported favourably on Kilmainham in terms of cleanliness, order and discipline, notwithstanding the unruly nature of the 'collection of convicts from the northern counties'. To this circumstance was attributed the failure of manufacturing employment within the prison. Thirteen years later little had changed, the 1836 report once again showing the prison to be satisfactory in terms of cleanliness but deficient in issues such as employment and appropriate accommodation for the 'minute classification' of the prisoners. Female prisoners were put under the care of a matron and were reportedly better clothed, instructed and employed than the male prisoners. They also benefited from charitable donations and visits from various ladies' committees. In contrast, no employment was provided for males save for the tread-wheel and breaking of stones for those sentenced to hard labour. Prisoners' diet, although economical, was judged sufficient and a medical officer of health engaged to attend to the sick. No accommodation was provided for turnkeys who were forced to live off-site, thus presenting a security risk in times of trouble. Most serious of all reported defects, however, was the insufficiency of accommodation in the prison. Sixty-two cells held over 100 prisoners and overcrowding became such a serious issue that in 1844 the Smithfield Penitentiary (see 2) was converted into a convict depot to relieve pressure by taking the troublesome convicts awaiting transportation to Australia.

East of the gaol is Kilmainham Court House built in 1820 to a design by Isaac Farrell. Located on the south-east corner of Inchicore Road and Kilmainham Bridge, the building is a solid two-storey composition with five bays, the three central bays advanced and crowned with a pediment surmounted with the royal coat of arms. The ground floor is rusticated and the main entrance door facing north is flanked by two blind doors. The central feature of the first floor is the three oblong round-headed windows below the pediment.

45. KILMAINHAM GAOL

Andrews, J.H. *A paper landscape: the Ordnance Survey in nineteenth-century Ireland*. Oxford, 1975; reprinted 2002.

Andrews, J.H. *History in the Ordnance map: an introduction for Irish readers*. Dublin, 1974; reprinted Kerry, Montgomeryshire, 1993.

Andrews, J.H. 'Ordnance Survey maps and manuscripts'. In Bernadette Cunningham and Siobhán Fitzpatrick (eds), *Treasures of the Royal Irish Academy Library*. Dublin, 2009, pp 201–11.

Bonar Law, Andrew and Bonar Law, Charlotte. *A contribution towards a catalogue of the prints and maps of Dublin city and county*. 2 vols. Dublin, 2005.

Boyd, G.A. *Dublin, 1745–1922: hospitals, spectacle and vice*. Dublin, 2006.

Casey, Christine. *Dublin: the city within the Grand and Royal Canals and the Circular Road with the Phoenix Park*. New Haven and London, 2005.

Casey, Christine (ed.). *The eighteenth-century Dublin town house*. Dublin, 2010.

Casserley, H.C. *Outline of Irish railway history*. Newton Abbot, 1974.

Clarke, H.B. *Dublin, part I, to 1610* (Irish Historic Towns Atlas, no. 11). Dublin, 2002.

Clarke, Peter. 'The Royal Canal 1789–1993'. In *Dublin Historical Record*, xlvi (1993), pp 46–52.

Close, Charles. *The early years of the Ordnance Survey*. London, 1926; reprinted Newton Abbot, 1969.

Coolahan, John and O'Donovan, P.F. *A History of Ireland's school inspectorate, 1831–2008*. Dublin, 2009.

Cox, R.C. *Bindon Blood Stoney: biography of a port engineer*. Dublin, 1990.

Craig, Maurice. *Dublin 1660–1860: the shaping of a city*. London, 1952; reprinted Dublin, 2006.

Cullen, Francis. 'Local government and the management of urban space: a comparative study of Belfast and Dublin, 1830–1922'. Ph.D., NUI Maynooth, 2005.

Cullen, L.M. *Princes and pirates: the Dublin Chamber of Commerce 1783–1983*. Dublin, 1983.

Curry, William. *The picture of Dublin or stranger's guide to the Irish metropolis*. Dublin, 1835.

Delany, Ruth and Bath, Ian. *Ireland's Royal Canal 1789–2009*. Dublin, 2010.

Dickson, David. *Dublin: the making of a capital city*. London, 2014.

Dublin delineated in twenty-eight views of the principal public buildings, accompanied by descriptions of each; with an itinerary, pointing out the leading streets, and principal objects of attraction. Dublin, 1843.

Dudley, Eugene. 'A silent witness: Cork Street Fever Hospital'. In *Dublin Historical Record*, lxii (2009), pp 103–26.

Fitzgerald, Garret. *Irish primary education in the nineteenth century* (Royal Irish Academy Monographs 2). Dublin, 2013.

Fraser, Murray. 'Public building and colonial policy in Dublin, 1760–1800'. In *Architectural History*, xxviii (1985), pp 102–23.

Gatenby, Peter. 'The Meath Hospital, Dublin'. In *Dublin Historical Record*, lviii (2005), pp 122–8.

Gilbart, J.W. *The history of banking in Ireland*. London, 1836.

Gilbert, J.T. *A history of the city of Dublin*. 3 vols. Dublin, 1854; reprinted 1978.

Gilligan, H.A. *A history of the port of Dublin*. Dublin, 1988.

Goodbody, Rob. *Dublin, part III, 1756 to 1847* (Irish Historic Towns Atlas, no. 26). Dublin, 2014.

Grierson, T.B. 'The enlargement of Westland-Row Terminus, with a sketch of the Dublin and Kingstown Railway, Part 1'. In *Transactions of the Institution of Civil Engineers of Ireland*, xviii (1888), pp 66–140.

Hall, F.G. *The Bank of Ireland, 1783–1946*. Dublin, 1949.

Hill, J.R. *From patriots to Unionists: Dublin civil politics and Irish Protestant patriotism 1660–1840*. Oxford, 1997.

Hourican, Bridget and Quinn, James. 'Sir Thomas Aiskew Larcom'. In *Dictionary of Irish Biography*. Cambridge, 2009.

Kirkpatrick, T. P. C. *The history of Doctor Steevens' Hospital, Dublin, 1720–1920*. Dublin, 1924; reprinted 2008.

Lennon, Colm. *Dublin, part II, 1610 to 1756* (Irish Historic Towns Atlas, no. 19). Dublin, 2008.

Lennon, Colm and John Montague. *John Rocque's Dublin: a guide to the Georgian city*. Dublin, 2010.

McAulay, Eve. 'Some problems in building on the Fitzwilliam estate during the agency of Barbara Verschoyle'. In *Irish Architectural and Decorative Studies: the Journal of the Irish Georgian Society*, ii (1999), pp 98–117.

McCullough, Niall. *Dublin, an urban history: the plan of the city*. Dublin, 2007.

SELECT BIBLIOGRAPHY

McGowan, Padraig. 'Money and banking in Ireland – origins development and future'. In *Journal of the Statistical and Social Inquiry Society of Ireland,* xxvi (1988/1989), pp 45–137.

McParland, Edward. 'Building the Parliament House in Dublin'. In *Parliamentary History,* xxi (2002), pp 131–40.

McParland, Edward. *Public architecture in Ireland, 1680–1760.* London, 2001.

M'Cready, C.T. *Dublin street names.* Dublin, 1892; reprinted 1987.

M'Glashan, James. *Dublin and its environs.* Dublin, 1850.

M'Gregor, J.J. *New picture of Dublin: comprehending a history of the city, an accurate account of its various establishments and institutions, and a correct description of all the public edifices connected with them.* Dublin, 1821.

Meenan, F.O.C. *St Vincent's Hospital, 1834–1994: an historical and social portrait.* Dublin, 1995.

Milne, Kenneth. *A history of the Royal Bank of Ireland, Ltd.* Dublin, 1964.

O'Boyle, Aidan. 'Aldborough House, Dublin: a construction history'. In *Irish Architectural and Decorative Studies: the Journal of the Irish Georgian Society,* iv (2001), pp 102–41.

O'Brien, Eoin, Browne, Lorna and O'Malley, Kevin. *The House of Industry hospitals 1772–1987: the Richmond, Whitworth and Hardwicke.* Monkstown, 1988.

O'Kane, Finola. '"Bargains in view": the Fitzwilliam family's development of Merrion Square'. In Christine Casey (ed.), *The eighteenth-century Dublin town house.* Dublin, 2010, pp 98–109.

Pearson, Peter. *The heart of Dublin: resurgence of an historic city.* Dublin, 2000.

Prunty, Jacinta. *Dublin slums 1800–1925: a study in urban geography.* Dublin, 1998.

Prunty, Jacinta. *Maps and map-making in local history.* Dublin, 2004.

Vaughan, W.E. and Fitzpatrick, A.J. (eds). *Irish historical statistics: population 1821–1971.* Dublin, 1978.

Warburton, John, Whitelaw, James and Walsh, Robert. *History of the city of Dublin, from the earliest accounts to the present time.* 2 vols. London, 1818.

Woods, Audrey. *Dublin outsiders: a history of the Mendicity Institution 1818–1998.* Dublin, 1998.

Wright, G.N. *An historical guide to the city of Dublin, illustrated by engravings, and a plan of the city.* London, 1825.

SELECT BIBLIOGRAPHY